DEBT-FREE BLUEPRINT

How to Get Out Of Debt and Build a
Financial Life You Love

LAURA D. ADAMS

What You'll Learn

Are you stressed about growing debt balances, out-of-control finances, and an uncertain future? Don't try to get out of debt without this book!

Debt-Free Blueprint: How to Get Out of Debt and Build a Financial Life You Love is an easy-to-follow guide to eliminate debt faster than you ever thought possible and create the financial future you deserve.

Award-winning author and top podcaster Laura D. Adams has helped millions of loyal fans grow rich with her savvy but down-to-earth and no-nonsense advice. Let Laura show you how to take control of your debt so you can stop worrying about money and build a life you truly love.

Debt-Free Blueprint walks you through the process of getting out of debt, using helpful examples and often-overlooked techniques, strategies, and programs. You'll learn how to make financial decisions with confidence and feel secure about your financial future.

In this book you'll discover how to:

- Get out of debt faster, even if you don't have extra money to make bigger payments
- Bridge the gap between your current reality and where you want your finances to be
- Create a simple but effective debt reduction plan that guides your life and keeps you focused
- Prioritize and tackle debt in the right order
- Settle and negotiate debt for less than you owe
- Stop making impulse purchases
- Optimize your debt so it costs less

- Use balance transfer offers to your advantage
- Refinance loans to save money
- Find government programs to make mortgages more affordable
- Make student loans fit into your budget
- Manage money stress so you achieve more and build a financial life you love
- And much more!

Debt-Free Blueprint is the book you need to get out of debt faster and for less out of pocket. If you like detailed tips, helpful examples, concise strategies, and inspiration from an extremely friendly and nonjudgmental teacher, then you'll love learning from Laura.

Praise for Laura

"Adams's peppy tone and highly organized, sensible advice deliver a clear-cut plan for financial literacy."

—*Publishers Weekly*

"I appreciate the resource materials and templates, the explanations were clear and very easy to understand. I feel empowered to take control of my finances."

—Deidre B.

"The thing I like about Laura's approach when it comes to managing your personal finances is that she gives you advice in bite-size chunks that are both easy to understand, and most importantly easy to implement."

—Lee C.

"I have been listening to the *Money Girl* podcast for a few years now, but this was very helpful in getting myself organized with all of the appropriate resources ... Debt is my biggest life stressor and I honestly feel more at ease. Thanks Laura!"

—Ashley D.

Connect With Laura

For more information about Laura's books, courses, podcast, and newsletter updates, visit: LauraDAdams.com

Connect with her on:

twitter.com/LauraAdams
bookbub.com/profile/laura-d-adams

Contents

Introduction	xiii

Section I
Assessing Your Finances

1. 13 Warning Signs That You Have a Debt Problem	3
2. Your Unique Financial Plan	13
3. Starting Where You Are Now	19
4. Getting the Big Picture of Your Finances	21
5. Identifying Your Assets	25
6. Identifying Your Liabilities	29

Section II
Making a Debt Reduction Plan

7. Tackling Debt in the Right Order	35
8. A System to Prioritize Your Debts	39
9. Settling and Negotiating Your Debts	45

Section III
Reducing Your Short-Term Debt

10. Consider Assets to Liquidate	55
11. Getting Rid of Credit Card Debt	59
12. 15 Ways to Kill Impulse Purchases	65
13. Optimizing Your Debts	77
14. Pros and Cons of Consolidating Debt	81
15. Using Balance Transfer Offers	89

Section IV
Reducing Your Long-Term Debt

16. Being Strategic About Long-Term Debt	95
17. What to Know About Refinancing	99
18. 5 Reasons to Refinance Your Mortgage	105
19. Using HARP to Refinance	111
20. Making a Mortgage Modification	115
21. Using a Mortgage Repayment Plan	119
22. Paying Down a Mortgage Early	123
23. Strategies to Pay Off a Mortgage Faster	129
24. Restructuring Student Loans	139
25. More Strategies for Managing Student Loans	145

Section V
Dealing With Old Debt

26. Understanding the Statute of Limitations for Debt	153
27. Should You Settle Old Debt or Pay It in Full?	157
28. 5 Debt Collections Rights You Should Know	163
29. Facts About Zombie Debt That Can Haunt You	169
30. Tips to Minimize Damage From a Late Payment	173

Section VI
Managing Money Stress

31. 7 Strategies to Reduce Money Stress	183
32. How to Stop Living Paycheck to Paycheck	193
33. Micro Habits That Create Financial Success	203
Maintaining Your Momentum	211
About the Author	215

Introduction

Can you *ever* get out of debt? The answer is yes, you can get out of debt! The time frame and priority for which debts to tackle first is different for everyone. The trick is creating a reasonable plan that you can stick with, and that's exactly what I'll help you do.

Since I became the host of the popular weekly *Money Girl* podcast in 2008 and an award-winning author in 2011, educating and motivating listeners and readers like you to take control of their debt has been an important part of my life.

When debt runs rampant in your financial life, it robs you of the ability to create a happy, comfortable future for yourself and your family. When you have debt under control, you can manage reasonable and affordable amounts—and still accomplish goals, such as retirement, putting kids through college, and owning a home.

I've had the honor of touching millions of lives through my writing, speaking, and consumer advocacy work. I've been featured thousands of times in media appearances and interviews for national TV, radio, print, and online outlets. One message that I continue to give is that you simply <u>can't save and build wealth for the future without cutting expensive debt.</u>

My personal mission is to help you get the knowledge, resources, and inspiration to manage money with confidence and create a richer life. So, I'm thrilled that you're reading these words or listening to the audiobook version.

I also want you to know that I've been exactly where you are today. You're probably frustrated and upset that you've accumulated either a little or a lot of debt and feel like you're drowning under the weight of it. You may not see a clear path back to financial health.

You might think that because I'm a personal finance expert and known as Money Girl, I've never struggled with debt. You might imagine that my finances have always been flawless and that I've never made a bad decision about money. Or maybe you think that I've never worried about how to pay off a growing credit card balance. Well, if you believe any of those things, you're dead wrong.

I feel fortunate to tell you that the days of my financial struggles are far behind me. But they're still etched in my memory. As a college graduate in my early twenties, I racked up some serious credit card debt that I carried right into my marriage. As we unpacked big cardboard boxes and started to fill our only bedroom closet, my husband asked, "So, exactly how many pairs of shoes do you have?"

It was obvious that my shopping habit would put a squeeze not just on our finances, but on our closet space as well. Over the next few years my husband and I piled some more debt right on top of our existing debt. We got extremely anxious about the growing credit card balance and made a commitment to each other to cut way back and slowly pay off the card. I'll never forget the feeling of accomplishment we had after making that final payment.

No one is immune from making financial mistakes, having poor judgment from time to time, or simply procrastinating doing what you know you need to do. The fact that you've downloaded this book means that you're ready to take responsibility for your financial health.

I know that once you get into financial debt, it's often easier to fall further behind than to dig yourself out. But no matter your situation, or how or why you got into debt in the first place, you can get out of debt.

If you're ready, I'll show you exactly how to do it.

SECTION I

Assessing Your Finances

1

13 Warning Signs That You Have a Debt Problem

Debt is a powerful tool that can help or hurt your finances depending on how you use it. Savvy consumers will leverage low-interest, and in many cases tax-deductible, debt to purchase assets that can appreciate over time, such as a home mortgage. Education debt can also pay off if it allows you to earn more over the long run—and it also comes with a tax break.

Never go into debt for anything that doesn't give you a return, including for consumer goods, dining out, or fancy vacations. Financing those types of purchases, especially on a high-interest credit card, causes you to lose wealth instead of building it.

tip: don't use credit card for: dining out, consumer goods

Expensive or excessive debt puts unnecessary strain on your finances that keeps you from making positive progress, such as building an emergency fund, investing for the future, and reaching your financial goals.

When you allow debt to get out of control, it causes a host of problems that ripple throughout your entire life, which you may be dealing with right now. Before we get into the nitty-gritty of how to get out of debt, let's take stock of some warning signs that you (or someone you know) may have a debt problem that should be addressed sooner rather than later.

1. You don't know what you owe.

If you don't know how many debts you have or their approximate balances, you need a reality check! If you're avoiding opening your bills or looking at credit card statements because you don't want to see the balances, then you already know you have a debt problem, and it's time to do something about it.

Hiding from a financial problem doesn't make it go away. Knowing where you stand with debt is the first step to getting it under control and improving your entire financial life.

If you're in the dark about your debt, we're going to shed light on it in the next few chapters. So, take the time to follow the plan that I outline in this book. I promise that any discomfort you feel about examining your debts and overall financial life will be well worth it.

2. Your debt-to-income ratio is too high.

Your debt-to-income (DTI) ratio is a key formula [→ saving capacity] expressed as a percentage that lenders use to evaluate you, and you can use it, too. To figure it out, add up your total monthly debt payments—including credit cards, loans, and your rent or mortgage payment—and divide that amount by your gross (pretax) monthly income.

For example, if you earn $5,000 and your debt totals $2,500 per month, your DTI is 50 percent ($2,500 / $5,000 = 0.5). Most lenders consider a DTI above 40 percent too high, especially when you're applying for a mortgage. So a 50 percent DTI means that you have more debt than you can handle for your income.

But even if you don't plan to buy a home or get a

large loan anytime soon, calculating your DTI is a good way to monitor your financial health. Download the free **DTI Calculator** at LauraDAdams.com/debt-toolkit to easily figure your DTI. Monitor your DTI to make sure that it decreases over time.

3. Your interest-to-income ratio is too high.

Another revealing ratio, your interest-to-income (ITI) ratio compares the total of your monthly interest charges on all your debts to your gross income. If it's more than 20 percent, take quick action to reduce it.

Paying high interest rates on debt means that you may not have enough left over each month to cover your basic living expenses, such as housing, food, and transportation.

Download the free **ITI Calculator** at LauraDAdams.com/debt-toolkit to easily figure your ITI and watch how this important ratio changes over time.

4. You can only make minimum payments on cards.

If you're stuck in a cycle of only paying the

tip: always pay more than the minimum in credit card payments.

minimum on credit cards each month, that indicates you have a debt problem. As interest accrues, you could end up paying double or triple the original cost of the items charged on the card.

For example, let's say you have a $5,000 card balance with an 18 percent annual percentage rate (APR) and a $100 minimum payment. If you only pay the minimum, it will take you over 30 years to eliminate the balance!

But if you stop making charges and pay $250 per month, you'd pay off the balance in under nine years. And paying $500 would allow you to eliminate the debt in just over four years.

5. Your credit cards are maxed out.

If you're using credit cards to satisfy a shopping habit or to buy necessities during a financial rough patch, you'll eventually hit your credit limit. You also may be charged fees if any purchases exceed your limit.

Even if you can pay more than the minimum payment each month, having a maxed-out card can cause your credit scores to plummet. If you're consistently using more than 20 percent to 30 percent of your credit lines, you probably have a debt problem that needs to be reined in.

6. You can't pay bills on time.

Tip: have calendar reminders!

If you're not paying bills on time, it could be because you're extremely unorganized. But it's more likely that your debt payments are more than you can afford to pay each month.

Ignoring bills may make you feel better in the short term, but I promise that they'll come back to bite you in the form of late fees and bad credit. Paying late only makes a debt problem worse.

Contact your creditors to discuss any financial hardship and ask for their help. You may be able to work out a payment plan to get caught up with past-due balances or have late fees waived. We'll talk more about negotiating with creditors in section 2.

7. You've borrowed to pay your bills.

If you have to borrow money from friends or family or take cash advances on credit cards, you certainly have a debt problem. Getting cash from a credit card is the worst way to use it because you're charged a higher interest rate than for regular purchases. Additionally, you're typically charged a cash advance fee.

Eventually, you'll run out of places to borrow and you'll have to face the balances you've racked up.

8. You overdraw your bank account.

I don't know too many people who have never accidentally bounced a check—even me. However, if you're paying expensive non-sufficient funds (NSF) fees on a regular basis, it's probably because you're spending more than you make and have a debt problem.

9. You don't have savings. *Warning: unexpected expenses*

Even people who aren't in debt can make the mistake of not saving. But if you've drained a savings or retirement account to pay off debt or to pay for everyday living expenses, that's when you know you have a debt problem.

If you don't have savings, you're living on the edge, financially speaking! Any unexpected expense could send you into a tailspin that causes you to go further into debt. Having cash on hand is the best way to avoid having to use debt in the first place. It's how you'll keep your head above water if you have a large unexpected expense or loss of income.

10. You've been turned down for new credit.

If you've recently been denied credit or can only qualify at a high rate, you may have poor credit, too much debt, or both. Review your credit using a free site such as CreditKarma.com or AnnualCreditReport.com to make sure there are no errors on your credit reports.

To learn much more about building and maintaining excellent credit, consider enrolling in my online class, ***Build Better Credit—The Ultimate Credit Score Repair Guide***, for a discount at LauraDAdams.com/debt-toolkit.

11. Your finances cause you to lose sleep.

If you're so worried about your debt and bills that you can't sleep at night, you certainly have a problem. Financial stress can lead to poor health, plus trouble focusing on your work.

Losing your job or business income is the last thing you need when you already have a financial problem.

12. You lie about your finances.

If you're lying to family or friends about your spending habits or how much debt you have, it's because you know deep down that there's a serious problem. If you're worried, losing sleep, and having trouble concentrating due to debt, it's time to take action using the plan in this book.

The only way to improve a bad situation is to be brave and face it. Denying a debt problem only makes it worse and prolongs your agony! The sooner you address it, the sooner you'll make positive financial changes.

13. You're getting calls from debt collectors.

When debt collectors start calling you, your debts are seriously delinquent and you have a big-time debt problem. If you don't face your past-due balances, you could end up in legal trouble. In section 5, we'll cover much more about how to deal with debt collectors the right way.

The good news is that if you recognize these warning signs, it's never too late to turn around your finances, pull yourself out of a debt hole, and have a brighter future. Are you ready to build a financial life you love? Let's get started!

RESOURCES: You'll find the free **DTI and ITI Calculators** (Excel) at LauraDAdams.com/debt-toolkit to understand and monitor your debt.

2

Your Unique Financial Plan

I know that getting out of debt is important to you. It's something you want to achieve to improve many aspects of your life. But first, I'd like you to take a step back and look at your financial life holistically and create an overarching financial plan.

Why is a financial plan important? Think of it this way: If you were building a new home, would you pour a concrete foundation before having finalized your house plan? That would be extremely risky and probably leave you with some major design flaws and regrets. <u>Creating a financial plan is just like having a detailed house plan—it shows what you intend to create with your money.</u> It's part of the process of identifying your goals and determining how you're going to manage your money to achieve them.

Financial planning may seem boring, but you just have to hunker down and do it if you want to make the smart moves necessary to live a financially secure life. It's possible to get lucky and end up having enough money to reach dreams, such as retiring with a big bank account or becoming debt free, by chance. But I wouldn't count on it!

Financial planning doesn't have to take a long time or be complex. You don't have to be a financial whiz or have a high-paying job in order to achieve your financial goals. Simply reflect on the big picture of your life. <u>What financial and non-financial dreams do you have</u>?

A useful exercise is to imagine your life five years from now. Consider where you're living and how you spend your time. In five years, what would you be proud to say that you had accomplished between now and then?

Stretch your imagination out further and do the same for your life in 10 or 20 years. Then imagine you're on your deathbed with just a few hours left to live. What accomplishments would make you feel good about yourself even in your final hours? These questions can give you important information about yourself and inspire you to begin planning for what truly matters to you.

This exercise will help you identify all your financial goals, big and small, so that you know what you're working toward. Then the rest of the book will help you achieve them by reducing your debt.

There are three different types of goals to consider when you're doing financial planning: short-term, medium-term, and long-term.

1. Short-term goals are those you want to achieve within a year. They could be getting out of credit card debt, maxing out a retirement account, or creating a holiday gift-giving fund, for example.

Two of the most important short-term goals that I recommend you achieve are establishing an emergency fund and substantially reducing or eliminating any dangerous debts you may have.

We'll talk a lot more about those debts and what strategies and tactics you can use to tackle them in upcoming chapters.

2. Medium-term goals are those you want to accomplish in the range of one to five years in the future. For many, a year isn't enough time to save up an adequate emergency fund, and so that objective might be a medium-term goal.

Other examples of medium-term goals that you may have in mind are making a down payment on a home, starting your own business, buying a new car, or saving for your children's education.

3. Long-term goals are, of course, those you want to achieve beyond five years into the future. The granddaddy of all long-term goals is saving for retirement. I'll give you tips on how to balance this while getting out of debt in a future chapter.

Download the free **Financial Planning Workbook** at LauraDAdams.com/debt-toolkit and set aside at least 30 minutes during a quiet part of your day to complete it. If you have a spouse or partner who shares your financial life or goals, you may want to complete your financial plan together. It's important to ask yourself crucial questions and then take the time to answer them as thoughtfully as possible.

* * *

RESOURCE: You'll find the **Financial Planning Workbook** (PDF) at LauraDAdams.com/debt-toolkit to create your unique goals for the future.

look it up!

→ 401(k) process for those starting a new job.
→ employer match
  ↳ how much to contribute

3

Starting Where You Are Now

I hope you were able to complete the **Financial Planning Workbook** with your current short-, medium-, and long-term goals. These are the dreams you have for yourself and your family, and they represent your personal values. Every financial move you make should get you a little closer to achieving those goals at some point in the future.

In this chapter, you'll learn an overview of the three steps you must take to improve your overall financial life. Improving your finances comes down to three steps:

1. Understanding what your financial situation is <u>today</u>

2. Knowing where you'd like your <u>future</u> financial situation to be

3. Acting on what needs to be done to bridge the gap between the two

today ⟶ future

The first step on any journey is to assess the situation. You have to be clear about where you are right now and where you want to go. So we're going to really assess where your finances are right now.

Being clear about your current financial situation can be difficult and even a little scary, especially if you're struggling with debt and don't want to face it. However, embracing reality makes you better able to make positive changes. Not facing reality may be part of the reason you've accumulated an uncomfortable amount of debt in the first place.

The first priority in assessing your financial situation is getting organized so you understand <u>your level of financial fitness</u>. In the next chapter I'll explain how to easily create an important tool to track the state of your finances throughout your life.

4

Getting the Big Picture of Your Finances

In the previous chapter, I mentioned an important tool to get organized and take stock of your financial situation. I call it your Personal Financial Statement, or PFS. It's critical for gauging your financial health because each time you update it, you calculate your net worth.

What exactly is net worth? you may be wondering.

The definition of net worth is summed up in a very simple formula: Net worth equals assets minus liabilities. Let me define what that means.

Your assets are things you own that have real value. Your liabilities, on the other hand, are the opposite of your assets. Liabilities are your financial obligations to others. When you subtract your total liabilities from your total assets, you've figured your net worth. It's really that simple.

Here's an example: If you own $200,000 in assets, but have $175,000 in debts, your net worth is $25,000. If you have $200,000 in assets and $200,000 in liabilities, your net worth is zero. And if you owe more than you own, such as $200,000 in assets and $250,000 in liabilities, your net worth is negative $50,000.

Since everyone's financial situation is unique, there's not a magic net worth number that you should have, but the <u>higher the better</u>.

[margin note: have specific metrics for NW]

Net worth is an important number because it reveals your bona fide financial resources at a given point in time. Tracking your net worth keeps you focused on increasing your assets and shrinking your liabilities, which is the key to building wealth. In this book, our focus is on how to reduce debt, or the liability side of the equation.

We'll cover exactly how to add your assets and liabilities to a PFS so you can calculate your net worth and really measure the health of your finances. I recommend updating it on a regular basis, perhaps annually or quarterly. It's the best way to get a complete view of your current situation and should be your financial "reality check"—something like stepping on the scale if you're watching your weight.

[margin note: calendar reminder.]

As you update your PFS in the future, you'll be able to track whether your net worth is increasing, flat, or decreasing. The goal is to slowly raise your net worth by reducing and eventually eliminating your non-essential debts. When you see your net worth increase slowly over time, pat yourself on the back and know that you're making the right financial decisions.

[margin note: NW = metric "the scale"]

I'll refer to your PFS quite a bit throughout this book, so be sure to create one. As I mentioned, it's a major touchstone that you'll use to understand your financial health and create your debt reduction plan.

Download the free **Personal Financial Statement** at LauraDAdams.com/debt-toolkit and complete it as you read the upcoming chapters.

* * *

RESOURCE: You'll find the free **Personal Financial Statement** (Excel) template at LauraDAdams.com/debt-toolkit to calculate your net worth.

5

Identifying Your Assets

In the previous chapter I recommended that you download the **Personal Financial Statement** spreadsheet. But you can also write down your information on paper or use a Google spreadsheet. Use any format that works for you and will be easy to update later on.

As a quick review, creating your PFS is so important for measuring and tracking your financial health because it allows you to easily calculate your net worth.

Net worth = total assets — total liabilities.

So let's cover how to identify and document your assets. Your assets are things you own that have real value, such as bank accounts, retirement accounts, real estate, vehicles, personal belongings, and money owed to you.

[Margin note: Use Software Personal Capital]

I'd like you to list every major asset you own on a separate row of the spreadsheet. Tab over to a column to the right and list each asset's estimated value. Or jot this down on paper.

Try to get as close as you can to an accurate value for each of your assets. However, you can always revise your estimated valuations at a later time.

For now, catalog your possessions and accounts that have monetary value. Then rank them from highest to lowest in value. For example, if your home is your largest asset, it would be at the top of your asset list.

Instead of taking a lot of time to list many smaller assets individually, try lumping them together in categories. Include a ballpark estimate for the value of your furniture, antiques, artwork, and collectibles, for example, under a category called "household possessions." Include computers and televisions under an "electronics" category.

The idea is to consider what you own that would have real value if you sold it today. Remember that the market value of most tangible assets is usually lower than their replacement value.

For example, if you paid $2,000 for your three-year-old computer or television, you could never sell it today for $2,000. So it's best to be conservative with your asset valuations on smaller or less expensive items.

For your larger assets, such as real estate, vehicles, boats, financial securities, or precious metals, spend some time researching their values for more accuracy. You could use a website like Zillow.com to understand the market value of your home. But remember that Zillow.com creates estimates from data available in the public records.

If you really want to know the market value of your property, it's best to hire a licensed real estate appraiser to do a thorough analysis. But Zillow.com may be a good starting point to find approximate values if you have real estate to include in your PFS.

If you have some expensive jewelry, that's another asset for which you may want the opinion of a qualified appraiser or gemologist.

Get the value of your investment or retirement accounts from your most recent statements. For vehicles, you might use Kelley Blue Book at KBB.com for current valuations. And sites like eBay.com and Craigslist.org can help you find going prices for assets like sporting equipment or high-end tools.

Once you've accounted for all your assets, create a "total assets" row and use a sum formula to add them up. In the next chapter we'll turn to your liabilities.

Identifying Your Liabilities

Now that you've entered all your assets in your PFS and know their total value, we're going to follow a similar procedure for your liabilities.

As I've mentioned, your liabilities are the opposite of your assets. Liabilities are your financial obligations to others. They could include a mortgage, a car note, credit card debt, or the $100 you owe your sister.

There are two different types of debt that you may have: installment loans and revolving lines of credit.

Installment loans, such as mortgages and auto loans, have specific conditions that must be met until the borrower pays off the full amount.

These loans are usually secured by an asset, such as real estate or a vehicle, and have an interest rate (either fixed or variable) and a term that specifies the future pay-off date. Installment loans are very different from revolving lines of credit.

Revolving lines of credit are very different from installment loans because the financial institution agrees to give you a maximum loan amount. They include credit cards and home equity lines of credit (HELOCs).

If you choose to use any part of the money, you're charged an annual percentage rate (APR) each month on the balance that you carry forward. The interest you owe each month is the minimum payment that you can make without incurring additional interest and late fees.

I'd like you to list each liability on a separate row in your PFS. Tab over to a column to the right and list the current balance for every loan, line of credit, credit card, and note that you have.

You may be able to get the necessary details by viewing your accounts online. If not, refer back to your most recent account statement or call the creditor for any missing information.

Also, your free credit report is a record of all your debts with creditors. You can get a free copy from a variety of places, such as CreditKarma.com and AnnualCreditReport.com.

Once you've entered all your debts, create a "total liabilities" row to see the grand total of all your debts. At the bottom of your PFS, create a "net worth" row using a cell formula that will subtract the total liabilities number from the total assets number.

Congratulations on completing your PFS! This is a big step in understanding where your finances stand today and seeing all your debt in one place. As I've mentioned, if your debt is larger than your assets, your net worth will be negative. But don't get too upset!

It's important to come to terms with how much you owe, even if it makes you uncomfortable. A sobering reality can help spark change.

In the next section, we're going to use all the information you've recorded on your PFS to make your personalized debt reduction plan so you know exactly how to begin to get out of debt.

* * *

RESOURCES: Use the free sites CreditKarma.com or AnnualCreditReport.com to review a record of your debts with creditors.

SECTION II

Making a Debt Reduction Plan

7

Tackling Debt in the Right Order

In the previous section, we focused on assessing your finances by creating goals (**Financial Planning Workbook**) and calculating your net worth (**Personal Financial Statement**).

For many people, both of those exercises can be difficult because facing your finances and totaling up all your debt can feel overwhelming.

I want to offer some words of encouragement if you're feeling upset or really struggling with debt right now. The best way to overcome a challenge is to meet it head-on. You *can* dig yourself out of debt. In my experience, the key to success is staying focused on finding solutions, not dwelling on problems.

Just like losing a lot of weight doesn't happen overnight, getting out of debt won't happen quickly, either. It's a part of making a commitment to a new and improved lifestyle. It's a part of accepting new beliefs about money and adopting better financial habits that you follow every day.

And don't let the desperation you may feel about your situation allow you to fall prey to get-out-of-debt-quick scams. Even those created by so-called nonprofits, who claim to have your best interests at heart, may not be legitimate. You'll conquer your debt by being persistent and chipping away at it bit by bit.

I want you to become the master of your money. Make a decision that you're going to control it, and not let it control you. Make a commitment to work proactively to improve your financial health every day. I'll help you create a solid debt reduction plan that will allow you to climb out of a financial hole, not slide back into one.

One of the questions I often hear about getting out and staying out of debt has to do with setting priorities. Many people are confused about which debts to tackle first and whether it's smart to eliminate all their debt.

I believe that there are good debts and bad debts—let me explain. Debt that allows you to make money is good. But debt that causes you to lose money is bad.

For example, an affordable home mortgage is generally a good debt because it allows you to buy a home that can appreciate in value over time. An auto loan is generally a bad debt (even though it may be a necessary one for most people) because vehicles depreciate quickly and rarely make money for the owner. You get the idea—going into debt for vacations, clothes, electronics, or furniture, for example, is not a wise investment in your future.

Believe me, I'm a strong proponent of keeping all debt as low as possible. But the issue isn't whether a mortgage or business loan is inherently a bad thing, because it isn't. The issue is whether you use a mortgage or a business loan to buy something that you can't afford in the first place. Buying a home that's way out of your price range is never wise.

The amount of debt that's acceptable for anyone is a highly personal evaluation. There are many factors to consider, such as future income, comfort level with risk, and net worth. If you have debt, but also have plenty of income to cover it, in addition to a sufficient emergency reserve fund, you probably don't have a financial dilemma.

But if you use debt to consistently finance a lifestyle that you can't afford, or if you're paying sky-high interest rates, it should be addressed sooner rather than later. If you have debt that's grown out of control or that weighs you down psychologically, now's the time to take swift action to repair the trouble.

So let's get started making your debt reduction plan. When it comes to getting out of debt, tackling your debts in the right order is key for success.

In the next chapter, I'm going to ask you to go back to your PFS to add some additional details for each of your liabilities. That additional information will allow you to prioritize your debts so you'll know exactly where to start.

A System to Prioritize Your Debts

The first step in getting a handle on your debt is to assess your overall financial situation by creating a Personal Financial Statement. So, if you haven't created it yet, take some time to gather up your information.

You should have each debt listed on a separate row in your PFS. In a column to the right, you should have the outstanding balance.

Now, I'd like you to add another column to the right of each balance that lists the interest rate. If you have debts with variable interest rates, you'll need to update your PFS with current information and reevaluate it on a regular basis, such as once a quarter.

Add another column to the right of your interest rates that lists the maturity or pay-off date for each of your installment loans. For your credit lines or credit cards, you can enter an "X" since there is no specified maturity date for those types of debt.

Now, I'd like you to add another column to the right and title it "pay-off priority." The interest rate, maturity date, and pay-off priority data will help you compare each of your debts objectively, based on the numbers.

In the previous chapter, I discussed the difference between good debt and bad debt. Here's another important differentiation that will help you prioritize which debts to tackle in what order: There are short-term and long-term debts.

Short-term debt has a maturity date less than five to 10 years in the future (or none at all, as with credit cards). They are the most dangerous debts—the ones I'll urge you to pay off first. They have the greatest potential and likelihood of really getting you into trouble.

Short-term debt can turn a slight problem into a bad one, and a bad problem into something absolutely devastating! In other words, time is of the essence for certain debts.

Long-term debt has a maturity date of 10 years or more from the date you took out the loan. Long-term debt is generally considered good debt. You shouldn't have excessive long-term debt for your level of income, but it has some redeeming qualities that make it not quite so dangerous.

Your long-term debt might include installment loans secured by assets, such as mortgages; debts that come with an allowable tax deduction, such as mortgages, home equity lines of credit (HELOCs), and student loans; and debt that could potentially raise your net worth, such as a business loan. Paying off long-term debts will fall lower on the priority scale.

Take a look at all of your liabilities on your PFS, and rank your top priority short-term debt as enemy number one. A debt that's owed to the IRS or due to litigation is very serious and must be wiped out first, because the government has more power over your life than anyone else you may owe. Therefore, the IRS can cause you the most misery if you don't settle your debts with them!

The next in line for elimination should be any loan or bill that's already in default, or in the hands of a collections agency, such as an unpaid medical bill, because delinquencies usually result in hefty late fees as well as bad marks on your credit report.

Your next highest priority debts should be payroll loans, vehicle loans, or credit accounts that charge the highest rates of interest. For example, a vehicle loan with 12 percent interest should be a higher priority than a credit card balance with a 10 percent interest rate. A small balance on a department store credit card that charges 18 percent interest should be paid off before a larger balance on a credit card with 14 percent interest, because on a percentage basis, higher-interest debt costs you more, and therefore should generally be ranked as a higher priority for elimination.

I want to make the point that in some cases short-term debt is not the result of unnecessary spending. Unpaid medical bills can pile up if you have to go without health insurance or get caught sick between jobs. Loans taken to purchase vehicles are one of the most important but worst investments most of us are forced to make for the sake of transportation.

I'm a realist. I recognize that having short-term debt can be something you don't choose to have. In some cases it's a lifeline to help you survive a real emergency such as the temporary loss of a job or business. Nevertheless, it's important to work hard at getting rid of the most toxic liabilities you have first, so they don't eat up your paycheck.

After you've prioritized your short-term debts, do the same for your remaining long-term liabilities. These might be student loans or mortgages. Again, use the interest rate as the indicator for pay-off priority.

For example, rank a home loan with a 10 percent fixed or variable interest rate as a higher priority than a 5 percent student loan. Now that you've organized your debt from highest to lowest priority, you have a clear plan.

In the next chapter you'll learn a tactic to handle any past due accounts you may have by settling and negotiating to pay less than you owe.

Settling and Negotiating Your Debts

Once you've paid down as many debts as possible with your existing assets and made attempts to lower your monthly obligations, you may still find that your debts are unmanageable.

First, scrutinize all your liabilities and check to see if you purchased or are currently paying for credit insurance. Credit insurance pays off a debt when certain situations occur, such as the loss of a family member who was providing income, or the loss of your job.

You may have been sold credit insurance as part of getting a loan and not even be aware of it. If you're paying credit insurance premiums, they'll be itemized on your loan or credit card statements. If so, request a copy of the policy and see if it applies to your current situation.

If any of your debts are past due, an often-overlooked tactic for reducing them is to settle for less than you owe. This will require you to contact those creditors or collections agencies directly.

If you have a large amount of past due debt, it may be worthwhile to speak with an attorney who specializes in debt and bankruptcy. Having an attorney review your finances and negotiate on your behalf may be worth the cost, depending on your situation.

However, for most people, it's easy to represent yourself. Yes, it may take some time and effort to negotiate delinquent debts, but it can really pay off.

It's been my experience that people who communicate quickly and honestly with creditors can get favorable treatment from them. I know that might sound daunting, but I promise that it can be easier than you think.

Many creditors are willing to reduce your debt significantly in order to get some amount of payment from you right away. The potential savings you can realize from negotiating a debt settlement is just too important to your financial health not to try it.

If you can pay some amount immediately or make a larger lump sum payment fairly soon, you're in a good position to negotiate with your creditors. The best debts to negotiate are unsecured debts, such as credit cards and medical bills, because they aren't backed by assets that the lender could sell.

So how do you begin a negotiation? First, never be intimidated or afraid to contact a creditor. They'll usually respond more kindly than you think they will. That's because the vast majority of people in debt try to hide from creditors instead of deciding to address their problems head-on.

There's no downside to negotiating because you can't get something unless you ask for it. Plus, you can't be punished with a higher interest rate or shorter repayment period.

Find a recent statement or go online to find the phone number for customer service. When you call, simply ask to speak to accounts receivable, the collections department, or a debt counselor. Different creditors and lenders have different names for the team or person who handles customer accounts.

Be polite but firm and clear about the fact that you're contacting them in an effort to settle or modify an outstanding debt. Don't get emotional. Remember that it's a business conversation for the person on the other end of the line. Be truthful about your situation, then let them do the talking.

Be sure to have a pencil and paper handy to take notes. Write down the:

- Creditor or agency name
- Date and time
- First and last name of the person you speak to
- Direct phone number
- Instructions or results from the call

If the creditor tells you right away that you can't settle your debt for less than the full amount, know that they're probably just negotiating with you, especially if the debt is old. Understand that it's extremely likely that they will take less money than they indicate.

Let the company know if you're in the process of speaking with other creditors and that you really want to work something out. Offer to pay 25 percent of the amount of the full debt that you owe. Perhaps they'll meet you in the middle at 50 percent of your debt.

Many credit card companies would be thrilled to get half of your debt right away rather than zero down the road. But if they won't budge, you shouldn't appear to be desperate to settle. Instead, try calling them back in a few days. It's likely that you'll speak to a different representative who may see the situation differently.

If after several attempts the creditor will not reduce the original debt amount, try requesting that all fees and interest be waived from the account. Always get revised terms on your debt in writing from the creditor or collections agency before you send any payments.

Medical debt can be challenging to untangle

because the billing and insurance system is so complicated. When you can't read or understand the lingo on a medical bill, it's easy for insurance mistakes to occur and for fraud to go unnoticed.

The Alliance of Claims Assistance Professionals at Claims.org may be able to help you verify the accuracy of medical bills you don't understand. They also offer advice on negotiating settlements with hospitals or other medical providers.

Generally you should approach negotiations for medical bills the same way as for other types of debt: Make an offer to pay off a percentage of your outstanding debt as quickly as you can.

But don't make the mistake of paying overdue medical bills with a credit card. Why? Creditors are likely to view medical debt with more sympathy than credit card debt. They may be more willing to work out a favorable payment plan for debt that's due to unforeseen medical problems versus for debt they assume to be the result of frivolous spending.

If you have past due medical debt, ask about hospital medical assistance funds and do some research at sites including:

- Centers for Medicare and Medicaid Services at Medicare.gov
- Guide to Government Information and Services at USA.gov
- State Health Department at HealthFinder.gov—may offer public assistance for those with medical bills who meet certain income, disability, or age requirements, depending on where you live

In section 5 five we'll cover more about the consequences of settling debt. You'll learn how it affects your credit, what it means for your taxes, and tips to complete a settlement the right way.

Now, on to section 3, where you'll learn specific strategies to eliminate different types of short-term debt you may have.

SECTION III

Reducing Your Short-Term Debt

10

Consider Assets to Liquidate

In this chapter we'll discuss how to reevaluate your assets in light of your short-term debts. So, your first task is to go back to your **Personal Financial Statement**. I told you that your PFS is an amazing tool that will help you take control of your finances!

I'd like you to review everything you entered in the assets section, such as cash in the bank, vehicles, sporting goods, collectibles, and so on. Many people like their assets so much that they're willing to keep them despite being over their heads in debt.

Do you have savings or investments that you can use to pay off your short-term liabilities? Do you see any items on your PFS that you could sell to raise cash? If so, paying off a 16 percent consumer debt on a credit card is just like finding an investment with a 16 percent rate of return that's tax free!

Now, I don't recommend selling or borrowing against retirement accounts to pay off debt, because the taxes and penalties for doing so are usually too high. Nor do I recommend using every penny of your cash to eliminate debt. It's still important to leave yourself a cash cushion that could keep you safe in an emergency situation, such as the loss of a job.

I understand that reducing a cash account or selling investments in a brokerage account to pay down your debt can be difficult. But you should always use your existing assets, outside of retirement accounts, to pay down short-term debts when you can—especially when they are dangerous debts such as:

- Past due child support
- Tax debts or liens
- Unsecured loans with sky-high interest rates, such as payday loans

- Maxed-out credit cards with double-digit interest rates

If you have existing cash that you can spare safely, non-retirement investments, unused vehicles with equity, or household items you can sell to raise cash, make a goal to liquidate them as quickly as possible.

Here are some great places to turn different types of unused or unwanted items into cash:

Clothes typically don't have much resale value. However, it may be worth selling special items, such as costumes, designer handbags, or vintage clothes on sites such as eBay.com, Etsy.com, or Craigslist.org.

For jewelry, first have your quality or antique pieces appraised, then sell them to a dealer, at auction, on consignment, to pawn shops, or through online sites.

If you have exceptional pieces of furniture, antiques, silverware, art, or collectibles, consider using an auction house, antique dealer, or Craigslist.org. For electronics, sporting equipment, and musical instruments, try

Craigslist, eBay.com, PlayItAgainSports.com, or pawn shops.

Have a yard sale on your own or with neighbors who can split advertising and set up costs to sell unwanted items—and then use the cash to pay down your top-priority debt.

Make a list of all the ways you can raise cash to make a dent in your short-term debt. Then carve out time each day to put those plans into motion.

In the next chapter, we'll focus on tactics to whittle down one of the most common short-term debts you may have: credit cards.

Getting Rid of Credit Card Debt

This chapter will help you get out of credit card debt, which often leads to deep financial trouble. Purchases made on bank credit cards and retail store cards can derail even the best financial intentions. No one seems to be immune from the perils of plastic—not the young, old, educated, uneducated, wealthy, or poor.

Credit cards are an equal opportunity threat because they're relatively easy to get. Even those with poor credit can often get a high-interest credit card—what a recipe for disaster!

Does that mean credit cards are evil? Absolutely not. The truth is, it's just a piece of plastic that happens to be a powerful financial tool. The problem with credit cards is that they can be accessories to a financially dishonest life—something you really can't afford.

Most short-term debt finances a lifestyle, rather than the purchase of genuine assets that hold their value over time. Once charges are made to a credit card, for example, what do you have to show for them?

You might have more clothes, furniture, gifts, electronics, or dinners out—which is all great stuff to buy if you can truly afford it. But it's likely that you spent money on something you really didn't need in the first place, and now that money is gone.

Many people think that it's okay to carry a credit card balance as long as they're making the minimum monthly payment. Please understand that just making the minimum payment isn't sufficient, because you're still accumulating interest on the balance you carry forward each month.

If your minimum payment is less than the interest charged each month, your credit card balance can actually still grow! It's kind of like

Getting Rid of Credit Card Debt • 61

getting stuck in quicksand—each effort forward seems to pull you back down.

Consider this medical analogy. The first rule for an open wound is to stop the bleeding, right? If we apply that first-aid treatment to credit card debt, your first mission is to stop making new charges. That doesn't heal the wound, but it stabilizes the patient.

Make a commitment to yourself that you will not make another purchase on the card, whatever it takes. So the trick to eliminating credit card debt is to stop charging and to make progressively larger payments at the same time.

One of the best ways to use a credit card as part of your money management system is to pretend that it's not really a credit card, but a debit card. That might sound like a silly mind game, but if it works, so what?

I want to point out that credit cards have a good side, too. As I mentioned, they're just a financial tool. For some, a credit card is a plastic invitation to reckless behavior. For others, responsible use brings nice rewards and benefits.

If you approach credit cards with discipline and

self-control, then you'll have a healthy lifelong relationship with them. Consider these benefits that can come with responsible credit card use:

Building up or improving your credit rating is very important for those just starting out. A good credit rating will open up a world of financial possibilities for you.

You can build or improve your credit rating by paying credit card bills on time and never maxing out your available credit limit. If your credit rating is less than perfect, demonstrating responsible credit card use is one of the fastest ways to improve your credit score.

Getting payment float time is when you make a purchase that you actually don't pay for until a later date. Credit cards typically give you a grace period of about 25 days. If you pay off charges made during that time, you're not charged any interest on a card.

For example, if you pay for a new television with a debit card, the funds are taken out of your account within a day or two. But if you pay with a credit card, you have a free grace period to submit payment.

Disputing charges is a perk that allows you to avoid having to pay fraudulent charges or dishonest merchants. That's why credit cards are a preferred method of payment for large purchases—plus, you can rack up some nice rewards.

Any defective merchandise or service problem that isn't resolved to your satisfaction can be taken up with the card's issuer. They'll work on your behalf to settle the issue and can suspend or reverse the charge on your account. Certain cards also offer built-in insurance for products or travel-related services.

Protecting your safety is a key benefit when compared to carrying paper checks or cash. The law is on the consumer's side when it comes to lost or stolen credit cards.

The Fair Credit Billing Act, established by the U.S. Federal Trade Commission, addresses these issues. It says that your maximum liability for unauthorized use of a credit card is $50. And if you have the card in your possession, but someone stole your credit card number, your liability is $0.

Make a goal to stop making new charges on your cards and to eliminate a set amount over a period of time. For instance, if you have $12,000 in debt, you could eliminate a minimum of $1,000 a month for a year, or $500 a month for two years.

Your extra savings in combination with serious belt-tightening, or even an extra source of income, is how you will triumph over a mountain of credit card debt. In the next chapter we'll review 15 ways to stop impulse purchases that may be at the root of your short-term debt.

15 Ways to Kill Impulse Purchases

No matter how frugal you are, no one is immune from making impulse purchases from time to time. But the more you give in, the more harmful it can be to your financial life.

Overspending is a common barrier to achieving key financial goals, such as saving for retirement or building an emergency fund. Spending more than you can afford, or buying things you simply don't need, can throw your financial stability off kilter.

Instead of caving to impulses, develop strategies that stand in the way between the compulsion to buy and buying. Use these 15 tips and tricks to resist bad spending habits so you can save more money:

1. Shop with a list.

Whether you're shopping for groceries, holiday gifts, or clothes, have a list of what you really need to buy and challenge yourself to stick to it. You'll always find something you didn't know you wanted, whether it's Oreos or designer shoes on sale.

Using a list as your shopping plan keeps you focused, so you're less likely to become distracted by anything that's not on the list.

2. Use a waiting period rule.

Create a rule that before buying anything over a certain amount, such as $50 or $100 you'll give yourself time to think about it. It could range from an hour to a month, depending on your propensity to splurge. But the longer you can wait, the better.

A good rule of thumb is to give yourself at least 24 hours to decide if buying something is a need, or just a random impulse purchase, by "sleeping on it." That allows enough time for your impulse to settle down so you can approach the purchase with a clear mind and decide if you really do need something.

If you're shopping in a brick-and-mortar store and find something that you think you can't live without, take a picture of it and its price. You can revisit the item after your waiting period has expired and even use the information to do comparison shopping online.

3. Calculate an item's value in time.

Since a spending impulse is often emotional, engaging the logical part of your brain is a powerful way to stop it. One tactic is to think about how much time it would take you to earn what an item costs.

For example, if you earn $25 an hour after taxes, buying a $250 suit costs you 10 hours of work. Is it worth the equivalent of a long workday? Only you can decide. Being a more logical shopper can instantly change your mindset so you think more rationally and put the brakes on an impulse purchase.

4. Don't buy anything that can't be returned.

Sometimes the most tempting purchases are the ones you can't return. Like a super-low final clearance price online that you think is too good to pass up. Sometimes there's a reason a marked-down item hasn't sold well, like not fitting well or being different from the picture.

We've all experienced how terrible it is to regret buying something you can't return. At least buying something you regret that you *can* return allows you to undo the damage, once you come to your senses.

5. Reevaluate what you already own.

If you're a compulsive shopper, you probably have a lot of stuff, such as a closet full of clothes or a garage full of gadgets that you rarely use. So, instead of buying the next item that you probably don't need, reevaluate what you already have.

Sometimes paring down is the key to figuring out what you really use so you can find more satisfaction in those items instead of accumulating more. I'm a big believer in buying fewer, but better-quality things.

Another strategy is to organize your belongings in better ways, so it's easy to see what you have. I really enjoyed arranging my closet and kitchen using the method made famous by Marie Kondo. Her techniques and mindset for approaching clutter have become a global phenomenon.

Check out her best-selling books:

- *The Life-Changing Magic of Tidying Up: The Japanese Art of Decluttering and Organizing*
- *Spark Joy: An Illustrated Master Class on the Art of Organizing and Tidying Up*

6. Plan your splurges.

If you're exceptionally prone to impulse purchases, trying to eliminate them altogether may be pointless. Instead, give yourself permission to make smaller purchases on a regular basis.

If you plan for one new inexpensive item a month, or a relatively expensive treat once a quarter, that can keep you from random binge buying. Setting aside a small amount of your budget as an impulse fund can give you a manageable and responsible outlet for spontaneous purchases.

7. Give yourself a no-spending challenge.

Set up a personal challenge that cuts impulse spending over a set amount of time. For instance, you might:

- Only buy essentials (such as groceries, housing, utilities, and insurance) for an entire month
- Cook at home every day for a month instead of eating out
- Not buy any new clothes for 60 days
- Wait at least 24 hours before buying anything more expensive than a certain dollar amount

Turning no-spend days into a game can make them easier to sustain and help you clearly identify spending triggers, such as surfing the web for clothes or dining out too frequently.

If cutting all frivolous spending is too intense, consider identifying categories that cause trouble, such as shoes or expensive cocktails, and cut them out during a period. Plan the best ways possible, such as cutting back on surfing the web or doing any window shopping.

Also put reminders of your challenge in strategic places, like a sticky note in your wallet or on your credit cards. If you slip up, just resume the challenge right away. You might even impose a good-cause penalty, such as matching any slip-ups as donations to your favorite charity.

8. Unsubscribe from retail newsletters.

The next time you see a retail newsletter in your email inbox with a tempting promotion or sale, look for the unsubscribe link at the bottom and break the cycle. Something you just happen to see on sale that you don't really need doesn't save money—it just hurts your financial life.

What's out of sight will be out of mind. That's one less way to spend money compulsively.

9. Only shop with a clear head.

Be sure to notice when and why you make impulse purchases. Are you sad, stressed, angry, tipsy, or all of the above?

You've probably heard the term "retail therapy." But there are many better ways to ease stress that don't involve spending money.

Even just being tired or hungry when you're shopping can be dangerous. Instead of thinking about a purchase logically, you just load up the cart and buy. Consider putting off shopping until another day when you're more rested and don't have a grumbling stomach.

Spending to boost your mood might work in the moment, but it really hurts you in the long run. It can lead to a vicious cycle where you're upset or stressed and buy something impulsively, then you get stressed further because you bought something impulsively!

Shopping in the evening can be a particularly bad time to make decisions if you're home alone, bored, or impaired after a few glasses of wine. So, remember never to shop when you're restless or having a bad day. Instead, call a friend, go for a walk, or take a hot bubble bath to cheer yourself up.

10. Never shop for entertainment.

If hitting the mall or main street shopping is hurting your finances, change your idea of entertainment. When you put yourself in the center of shopping temptations, you're probably going to buy something.

So, stay away from outlets or your favorite stores when you have time to kill and need to curb impulse buying. And don't hang out with friends whose lives revolve around shopping when it just isn't in your budget.

When you really need something, shopping solo can be a more mindful experience that keeps you more in control and calm compared to the chaos of shopping with friends or kids.

11. Read the reviews.

The next time you're tempted to buy something, read all the product reviews you can, especially the low ones. Oftentimes bad reviews are exaggerated claims, but sometimes they show you the truth about the bad side of a product that may make you realize that it's not worth buying.

12. Abandon the shopping cart.

When you find yourself in a situation where you're about to give in to a buying impulse online, try putting the item in your cart, but then leave the site. In some cases, choosing the product may be enough to satisfy your urge to shop—even if you don't go through with the purchase.

13. Minimize the damage.

If you're in a store and feel like you're overcome with the desire to buy lots of stuff, consider taking one inexpensive item to the checkout and get out of the store with minimal financial damage. It's not an ideal habit to follow, but stopping while you're ahead may be a way to ease away from shopaholic tendencies.

14. Think about the last purchase you regret.

Before you pull the trigger on your next shopping impulse, think about the last time you made a buying decision that you regret. That may reveal a pattern in your behavior that you want to squelch.

Decide that you won't let yourself make another bad impulse purchase today that you'll be sorry for in the future.

15. Remember your goals.

The idea behind curbing impulsive spending is so you can use that money to achieve your most cherished financial goals instead. So, remember the goals you created in chapter 1, using the **Financial Planning Workbook**.

Consider summarizing your goals on one or more index cards or sticky notes and keeping them in strategic places you can't avoid if you choose the wrong path.

For instance, you could put a summarized reminder on your refrigerator, desk at work, or bathroom mirror. Use it as a screen saver for your mobile devices and computers. Or use a Sharpie pen to write your goals on your debit and credit cards.

Creating visible triggers that prompt you to think about what you want to accomplish can be a powerful way to sidestep destructive financial behaviors. Any strategy you can use to keep your goals top-of-mind will help you focus on what's most important and reinforce your commitment to get out of debt. Your goals will guide your behavior, but only if you remember them.

The best way to resist any impulse is to put time between the impulse and the action. So the more time you give yourself to settle down, remember your goals, and reconsider the purchase, the easier it becomes to resist.

13

Optimizing Your Debts

If you can't pay off a debt with your existing assets or negotiate a settlement for less than you owe, this chapter will teach you how to optimize debt. Optimizing is any strategy that allows you to reduce your interest rates and fees on a debt until you can pay it off.

Shifting debt from higher-interest accounts to lower-interest options is a powerful way to optimize. It doesn't make your debt disappear, but it does reduce your interest expense.

Optimizing can help you get some financial breathing room or have more money to pay toward your debt each month. See what resources you already have that you're not using to pay off debts or to shift balances so they cost less until you can eliminate them.

For instance, do you have a low-interest home equity line of credit (HELOC) that's large enough to accommodate balances you can transfer from higher-interest credit cards or loans? How about a friend or relative who's willing to offer you a low-interest loan that you pay back over a few months?

Another way to save money on monthly debt payments is to consolidate it using a personal loan. A consolidation allows you to lump together two or more debts into one new, larger loan. The lender pays off your existing loan or debt balances and replaces them with a single loan, so you have just one lender to pay.

You can get a personal loan at most banks, credit unions, and a variety of online lending companies. The amount you can borrow depends on the lender, your credit, and your income.

Personal unsecured loan amounts usually range from $500 to $35,000 and have a fixed interest rate. If you want to borrow more, you typically have to apply for a secured loan.

Personal loans come with a choice of repayment terms that may range from three to 10 years. If you want to pay off a personal loan ahead of schedule, most don't charge you a prepayment penalty.

However, most personal loans come with an origination fee that could range from 1 percent to 10 percent of the loan amount. This is a one-time fee that is deducted from your loan proceeds.

You may see an initial interest rate when you apply, but a higher rate when you're quoted. This is because the fee must be included in the annual percentage rate (APR) for the loan you choose.

That means one lender that seems to have a lower APR may actually be more expensive if it charges a higher origination fee than another lender. So do your homework by shopping and comparing interest rates with multiple lenders.

When you're approved for a personal loan, you'll receive a check or a direct deposit into your bank account within days. Then you make regular monthly payments, just like you do with other types of installment loans, such as a car loan or home mortgage.

For each loan payment you make, a portion goes toward the principal amount you borrowed and a portion goes toward the interest owed on the outstanding balance.

If you can pay more than your monthly payment, make sure the lender knows to apply it toward your principal balance. Otherwise they may hold it in an escrow account or put it toward future interest payments, instead of using it to decrease the amount you owe. This is important because paying down your principal balance sooner means that you'll pay less interest over the term of the loan.

In the next chapter I'll review the main pros and cons of consolidating debt using a personal loan that you should consider.

14

Pros and Cons of Consolidating Debt

If you have a manageable amount of debt that you want to eliminate, debt consolidation is an easy way to optimize it. Here are five main benefits of using a personal loan to consolidate debt:

1. Paying a lower interest rate.

Cutting your interest expense is the primary reason to consolidate debt in the first place. Let's say you have a $10,000 balance on two credit cards. If one charges 18 percent and one charges 10 percent, paying them off with a loan that charges 9 percent will save you money.

High interest rates are one of the reasons many

people stay in debt longer than they should. It is wise to reduce the cost of your debt so you can eliminate it faster.

2. Getting fixed terms.

Personal loans are a type of installment loan, which means you have a specific interest rate and term, such as paying 9 percent for three years with monthly payments of $750.

If you've gotten out of control with credit card spending, having the discipline of a set term might help you pay off debt faster. Of course, be sure that the repayment term is affordable. Never commit to a payment schedule that you can't meet.

In general, the shorter your term, the higher your monthly payment. Having a longer term cuts your monthly payment—problem is, it also increases the amount of interest you'll pay over the life of the loan.

So I recommend choosing the shortest repayment period that you can reasonably afford.

3. Having one payment.

Consolidating multiple debts with a personal loan can simplify your financial life. You'll only have to keep track of one bill due date instead of several.

You can focus all your time and attention on making that single payment, counting down the months until your debt is completely wiped out.

4. Reducing your monthly payment.

Using a personal loan to consolidate debt can lower your total monthly payments.

For example, if the total of your minimum credit card payments is $500 and your new loan payment is $400, you have an additional $100 each month to pay down your loan's principal balance even faster.

But this will depend on how you structure your loan. As I mentioned, the shorter the term, the higher your monthly payments will be.

5. Building credit.

Having an additional loan on your credit report will help you build credit, if you make payments on time. Plus, paying off or reducing your credit card balances can boost your credit by lowering your utilization ratio.

To learn more about this topic, read or listen to episode 467 of the *Money Girl* podcast, "5 Lesser-Known Reasons Why Your Credit Score Drops."

You'll find the full archive of podcasts in the Money Girl section at QuickAndDirtyTips.com.

Download the free **Credit Utilization Ratio Calculator** at LauraDAdams.com/debt-toolkit to easily figure your credit utilization ratio.

HERE ARE three main negatives about using a personal loan to consolidate your debt:

1. Continuing to use credit cards.

Doing a consolidation should be part of a bigger plan to pay off debt. If you use a personal loan to pay off your credit cards, but then rack them back up, you've gotten deeper into debt. So you must be committed to never carry credit card balances again.

Those clean cards can be awfully tempting! Make

sure you get a fresh start by only making charges that you can pay off in full each month.

If you continue to accumulate debt, it doesn't matter how many times you move it around to lower interest options, it will continue to be a drag on your finances and keep you from building wealth.

So know your own capabilities and financial habits, and be honest with yourself. If you don't have the discipline to use your credit cards wisely after a consolidation, lock them up and only spend cash.

2. Having higher monthly payments.

While monthly payments for a personal loan can be lower than the total of all your minimum credit card payments, they can also be higher. As I previously mentioned, the payment amount depends on how much you borrow, your interest rate, and the loan length.

Unlike a credit card where you can make a minimum payment, with a personal loan you're required to make the full payment every month. If you pay late, you can destroy your credit.

3. Saving too little.

If your debt is relatively small or you can pay it off within the next 12 months, using a personal loan to consolidate may not save you enough to be worthwhile.

When you know that you can pay off a credit card or loan in the near future, but still want to cut the interest, consider using a zero interest balance transfer credit card. We'll cover more about balance transfers in the next chapter.

To sum up, optimizing debt with a personal loan is a smart financial tool to use if it's the least expensive option for you to consolidate debt. While it may seem odd to use new debt to get out of old debt, it all comes down to the interest rate. By using a personal loan the right way, you can reduce your interest payments and get out of debt faster.

* * *

RESOURCES: On the toolkit page at LauraDAdams.com/debt-toolkit you'll find the free **Online Loan Comparison Chart** (PDF) with the best places to shop and compare personal loans.

You can also download the free **Credit Utilization Ratio Calculator** (Excel) to figure your credit utilization.

15

Using Balance Transfer Offers

In this chapter you'll learn how to use a balance transfer offer to optimize your debt wisely. These are commonly included on credit cards as an incentive to move debt from an account (such as another credit card or an auto loan) to the card. It allows you to pay 0 percent or a very low interest rate during a promotional period, which typically ranges from six to 24 months, giving you a nice break from interest charges.

Transferring debt from a higher-interest account to a credit card that charges no interest can save a substantial amount of money. The amount you can transfer is subject to the credit limit you're offered. Additionally, there's usually a one-time transfer fee in the range of 2 percent to 5 percent for amounts you move to a transfer card.

Doing a balance transfer is a good strategy if, and only if, you know for sure that you can pay off the balance in full by the offer's expiration date. If not, the resulting interest rate could be higher than what you're currently paying. Here's a situation where doing a balance transfer makes sense:

Let's say you're having a good year at work and are going to receive a $5,000 bonus within six months. You plan to use the bonus to wipe out your $4,000 credit card debt. Instead of waiting for the bonus, you can pay off the balance with a transfer offer for 0 percent interest for six months.

Assuming a monthly interest charge of $100, you'd save $600 over the promotional period. Once you receive your bonus, you'd pay off the transfer card in full, before the 0 percent offer expires.

But if you're not positive that you can pay off your full balance in time, don't risk doing a balance transfer. When the music stops playing and the low rate ends, you might get stuck with a high interest rate and few options to improve the situation.

You could try to transfer the debt to another low-rate card right away, but if you're not approved for one, all the savings you had hoped to gain from doing a balance transfer would be lost. You'd probably be worse off than if you hadn't done a balance transfer in the first place. So always have a solid exit strategy for paying your balance off before the promotional rate on a balance transfer card disappears.

Before you pull the trigger on doing a transfer on a current or new card, make sure that you understand all the card terms. Be extremely cautious; there are severe penalties buried in the fine print that can sneak up on you.

For example, one late payment on most balance transfer offers results in a rate hike into the stratosphere. You must continue making minimum payments. If you miss a due date, default rates can go as high as 29.99 percent! Yikes!

Here are important features of transfer credit cards to evaluate:

- The interest rate charged for transfers made during the promotional period
- The interest rate charged after the promotional period (That's only important, of course, if you don't pay off the card in full or if you plan to use the card afterward.)
- The duration of the low-rate promotional offer
- The balance transfer fees
- The annual card fee

Good places to shop for transfer cards include CreditCards.com and Bankrate.com. Look for one with no annual fee, the lowest transfer fee, and the lowest promotional rate that lasts the longest period of time. Always apply the savings to your principal balance so you can get out of debt faster.

In the next section you'll learn specific strategies to eliminate different types of long-term debt you may have.

SECTION IV

Reducing Your Long-Term Debt

16

Being Strategic About Long-Term Debt

Now that you've created a debt reduction plan and have strategies to deal with your top-priority, short-term debts, you're in a position to deal with the less dangerous ones. In this section we'll cover how to reduce your long-term debt.

Long-term debts, such as mortgages and student loans, are as common today as blue jeans. That's because even the average price of a home and the cost of a basic college education are out of reach for most. These high-ticket items become affordable only when the price is stretched out over many years.

If the principal amount borrowed and interest rate of long-term loans are reasonable, then the monthly payment can remain manageable for most people who have steady incomes. Your job in this section of the book is to consider all the alternatives for your long-term debts.

Just like with your short-term debts, rank your long-term debt according to interest rate. For instance, rank a 5 percent student loan as a higher priority than a 4 percent mortgage. A lower interest rate makes the debt less expensive and therefore more tolerable.

Whether you'll take an allowable tax deduction on a loan is an important consideration because the tax savings reduces the after-tax interest rate you pay. Mortgages, home equity lines of credit (HELOCs), and student loans all come with tax deductions for taxpayers who are eligible.

That means if you claim a home mortgage interest tax deduction, the after-tax rate on a 4 percent mortgage could actually be closer to 3 percent, making it lower on your priority scale.

The challenge is to reduce your long-term debts without jeopardizing your ability to pay down your short-term debts. There's a balance between lowering your long-term costs and saving money in the short-term to pay off your pressing debts.

You don't want to have long-term debt forever. But make sure that you give short-term debt your full attention first. Then focus on optimizing and paying down long-term debt more aggressively.

In the next chapters you'll learn how refinancing can be a smart way to manage long-term debt.

What to Know About Refinancing

Refinancing is a fundamental way to pay less for certain types of debt. Most types of installment loans, such as for houses, cars, and education, have the potential to be refinanced.

Doing a refinance means your old loan is paid off and a completely new loan is created with new terms, such as a reduced interest rate and lower, fixed monthly payments. It's a powerful tool that can be used to your benefit in a variety of situations. I'll just refer to mortgage refinances here because they're the most common type.

First, there are two types of mortgage refinancing options available:

1. Traditional refinancing is available through your existing lender or another lender, if you qualify.

2. The **Home Affordable Refinance Program (HARP)** is a federal program designed to help homeowners who don't qualify for a traditional refinance. We'll discuss HARP in an upcoming chapter.

With a traditional refinance, you go through an application, approval, and closing process, similar to when you got your original mortgage. The lender verifies your income, debts, credit score, property value, and more. If your credit rating has improved since the time you took the original loan, that will help you get the lowest interest rate possible.

It's important to understand that doing a traditional refinance can be expensive. Even mortgages that are advertised as being "no-cost" or "low-cost" always have fees hidden somewhere. Any time you get a new loan there are fees that have to be paid to the lender as well as to other parties involved in the transaction.

In other words, you must carefully weigh the total costs against the long-term savings or benefits you'd receive from doing a refinance. Typical closing costs for a refinance could be as high as 3 percent to 5 percent of the outstanding loan amount or more.

Refinancing fees vary depending on the location of the property and the lender, but they should be similar to or less than the costs you paid for the original loan. You may be able to finance closing costs by adding them to your new loan amount.

However, when you "roll" closing costs into a loan, not only does the amount you borrow increase, but so may the interest rate you pay for the life of the loan. For that reason, it's best to pay loan closing costs up front when you can, instead of borrowing them.

Here's an important tip: Always evaluate the long-term savings you can get by paying loan closing costs up front. Ask the lender for a side-by-side comparison of principal loan balances, interest rates, and monthly payments for each loan option.

If you plan to refinance a mortgage, it's best to start by contacting your current lender. They'll probably want to keep your business and may be willing to give you a favorable interest rate or to eliminate some of the typical refinancing fees like the application or origination fee.

To do a traditional refinance, you must have a loan-to-value (LTV) ratio that falls within the lender's guidelines. What's an acceptable LTV ratio varies from lender to lender. They'll require a new or fairly recent appraisal of your property to make their calculation.

Here's how to estimate your LTV:

1. Find out how much your property is approximately worth (Zillow.com can help).

2. Find out how much you currently owe on the property.

3. Divide the loan amount (#2) by the value amount (#1).

Here's an example to consider:

Amy and Alan want to refinance their $250,000 mortgage on their vacation river house to take advantage of reduced interest rates. Their lender requires an LTV that does not exceed 80 percent to do a refinance.

The market value of their property is estimated to be $300,000. So their LTV is $250,000 divided by $300,000, which equals 83 percent. Unfortunately, that exceeds the lender's 80 percent LTV requirement and their refinance application is denied.

To know if the cost of doing a refinance is worth it, you need to know the financial break-even point (BEP). A refinance BEP occurs when you fully recover your costs and start to benefit from the refinance.

The BEP depends on various factors, such as the old and new loan interest rates, closing costs, your income tax bracket, how long you plan to own the home, and any loan prepayment penalties you have to pay. If you sell the property prior to reaching the BEP, there's no benefit to doing a refinance because you'd spend more than you'd save.

If you're not sure what your refinance BEP

would be, ask potential refinance lenders to help you make the calculation.

In the next chapter you'll learn specific reasons why refinancing a mortgage can make sense.

5 Reasons to Refinance Your Mortgage

There are a variety of situations when refinancing your mortgage can help improve your overall financial life. Here are five reasons you may want to refinance:

1. Convert to a fixed-rate loan.

A fixed-rate loan gives you a predictable monthly payment that can't increase. That's different from how other types of mortgages work, such as the adjustable-rate and interest-only mortgage.

Non-fixed-rate loan payments can increase when interest rates go up, which means you pay more interest on the balance of what you owe. A fixed-rate loan may have a larger monthly payment than other options; however, it can still save you a bundle in interest over the life of the loan. Have a lender do a side-by-side comparison for you, so you can compare total costs.

2. Lock in a lower interest rate.

If you find that the interest rate for your type of loan has dropped, you should always run the break-even numbers for doing a refinance. Take the time to investigate the potential benefits of refinancing any long-term installment loan when interest rates are decreasing.

Sometimes we get fooled into thinking that small changes in interest rates aren't worth the hassle of doing a refinance. A good rule of thumb is to investigate doing a refinance whenever the interest rates have dipped approximately 1 percent below your current rate.

Here's an example to help you see how small changes in interest rates can make a huge difference over the life of a long-term loan such as a mortgage:

Sarah bought a house for $200,000 with a 5 percent down payment. She put $10,000 down and mortgaged the remaining $190,000.

Her loan is to be repaid over 30 years at a 6.75 percent fixed rate of interest. That means she'll pay a whopping $253,641 just in interest over the life of the mortgage! That doesn't even include the $190,000 in principal she has to repay.

If interest rates for 30-year fixed-rate mortgages go down to 6 percent from 6.75 percent, should Sarah consider doing a refinance? Let's see.

If Sarah refinanced the loan for 30 years at the new interest rate of 6 percent, by comparison she'd pay $220,092 in interest. That's a savings of $33,549 in interest over the life of a 30-year loan. The "refi" would reduce her monthly payment from $1,232 to $1,139, giving her a monthly savings of $93.

At first glance a savings of $93 per month seems great, but as I mentioned, doing a refinance also costs money. Assuming her closing costs are equal to 3 percent of the $190,000 loan balance, that comes to $5,700.

In order to break even and make the refinance worthwhile, Sarah would need to keep her refinanced loan for a little more than five years. I calculated this break-even point by diving her total refinancing cost by her monthly savings: $5,700 / $93 per month = 61 months.

After 61 months, Sarah's savings from doing a refinance would be greater than the cost.

You can use the **Mortgage Refinance Calculator** at LauraDAdams.com/debt-toolkit for help crunching the numbers for your situation.

3. Lower your monthly payments.

A common goal of refinancing is to save money with lower monthly payments. The lender does that by extending the maturity date of the debt, reducing the interest rate, or both. A good strategy for the savings you might receive from doing a refinance is to use it to make extra payments on your highest-interest (most expensive) debt and pay it down faster.

You must be clear about what you're trying to accomplish from doing a refinance and carefully weigh the pros and cons. If you run a break-even calculation and find that the long-term savings will offset the costs related to a refinance, it's probably worthwhile. If you can put the savings to good use or can invest the savings wisely, you'll come out ahead.

4. Manage a balloon payment.

A balloon payment is a large payment that's due at the end of a loan. For example, you might borrow $300,000, but have monthly payments based on just $100,000 for a 10-year period.

The remaining $200,000 would be due as a final payment to the lender at the end of the 10-year term. Since most borrowers don't have the ability to fully pay off a large balloon payment, they choose to refinance.

5. Cash out equity you've built up.

Taking equity out of a home by doing a refinance can be a bad idea if you spend it on a Caribbean vacation. Squandering equity on anything that won't increase your net worth is detrimental to your financial health.

But cashing out equity can be a smart idea if you use the money for an alternate investment that appreciates in value or will make you more money than you have to pay in interest.

In the next chapter I'll review how to make a

mortgage more affordable by using an available federal program known as HARP.

RESOURCE: Use the free **Mortgage Refinance Calculator** at LauraDAdams.com/debt-toolkit to find out if you should consider refinancing your mortgage.

19

Using HARP to Refinance

The Home Affordable Refinance Program, or HARP, is unique. It's the only refinance program that allows homeowners who are current on their payments, but have little to no equity in their homes, to refinance.

HARP was created in 2009 in response to the recession and its housing crisis. As home values declined rapidly, many borrowers were "underwater," owing more than their property was worth. It became unaffordable to sell your home and impossible to refinance it.

The HARP offering has evolved, but it is currently set to expire at the end of 2018. However, Fannie Mae and Freddie Mac, which are government agencies, will offer permanent refinance programs for eligible borrowers with high loan-to-value loans. This will fill the gap HARP leaves behind at the end of 2018. Visit HARP.gov for up-to-date information.

The bottom line is that if your mortgage is owned by Fannie Mae or Freddie Mac, you may qualify for HARP or another refinancing program. That could save thousands with a lower rate or other more favorable terms. No minimum credit score is required and closing costs can be bundled into the new loan so you don't need much cash up front.

HARP may be an option if:

- You have had a good payment history for the past 12 months
- Your home is your primary residence, second home, or investment property
- Your home value has decreased
- You have limited equity or your first mortgage exceeds the current market value of the home
- Your loan-to-value ratio is greater than 80 percent

- Your loan is owned or guaranteed by Fannie Mae or Freddie Mac (check the Fannie Mae Loan Lookup tool at KnowYourOptions.com/loanlookup)
- Your loan was closed on or before May 31, 2009 (this date can be found using the loan lookup results)

Top reasons to refinance with HARP:

- Lower your monthly payment
- Reduce your interest rate
- Get a fixed-rate mortgage that won't change over time
- Build equity faster—shorter-term options may be available
- Save time and money with usually no appraisal required

HARP includes:

No underwater limits. Borrowers will now be able to refinance regardless of how far their homes have fallen in value. Previous loan-to-value limits were set at 125 percent.

No appraisals or underwriting requirements.

Most homeowners will not have to get an appraisal or have their loan underwritten, making their refinance process smoother and faster.

Modified fees. Certain risk-based fees for borrowers who refinance into shorter-term loans have been reduced.

Less paperwork. Lenders now need less paperwork for income verification, and have the option of qualifying a borrower by documenting that the borrower has at least 12 months of mortgage payments in reserve.

Program deadline. The end date to get a HARP refinance is December 31, 2018, but the deadline may be extended.

There is a quiz at KnowYourOptions.com to find out if you qualify for HARP.

In the next chapter I'll cover more ways to make a mortgage more affordable.

Making a Mortgage Modification

In addition to a traditional refinance and HARP, consider using a mortgage modification to make your home loan more affordable. With a modification, you reach an agreement with your lender to change the original terms of your mortgage.

A modification is basically a refinance that's both easy and free because the lender pays all fees to process the paperwork. If your income has been substantially reduced or if you don't have funds available to do a typical refinance, you may be a perfect candidate for a modification.

The lender will ask you to submit your income and expenses on an application. They review your information to determine if the loan payment is too high for your current income.

A modification involves one or more of the following:

- Changing the mortgage loan type, such as changing an adjustable-rate mortgage to a fixed-rate mortgage
- Extending the term of the mortgage, such as from a 30-year term to a 40-year term
- Reducing the interest rate either temporarily or permanently
- Adding any past due amounts, such as interest and escrow, to the unpaid principal balance

A modification may be a good option if:

- You can't get approved for a mortgage refinance
- You're facing a long-term hardship
- You're several months behind on your mortgage payments or likely to fall behind soon

There are many benefits of doing a mortgage modification, including:

- Making your new loan current, which resolves a delinquency status if you're behind on payments
- Reducing your monthly mortgage payments to a more affordable amount
- Changing the original terms of your mortgage permanently, giving you a new start
- Damaging your credit less than getting forced into a foreclosure
- Staying in your home and avoiding foreclosure

If you have a Fannie Mae mortgage, you may qualify for a Flex Modification. This program replaces the Home Affordable Modification Program (HAMP), which ended in 2016.

As we covered in the previous chapter, you can use the Loan Lookup tool at KnowYourOptions.com/loanlookup to see if Fannie Mae owns your loan.

The benefits of a Flex Modification include:

- Lowering your mortgage payment by as much as 20 percent
- Adding any past due amount to the unpaid loan balance so you won't have to pay it up front
- Making your home loan current (once you complete a modification trial period plan and execute modification documents)
- Helping you avoid foreclosure and stay in your home

In the next chapter I'll cover another strategy to make a mortgage more affordable.

Using a Mortgage Repayment Plan

Another strategy to manage a mortgage that's become unaffordable is entering into a repayment plan. This allows you to spread out your past due amount over several months, such as a three-, six-, or nine-month period, to get current.

A repayment plan may be an option if:

- You are ineligible for or don't want to do a refinance or modification
- You are facing a short-term hardship
- You are several months behind on your mortgage payments
- You can now afford your monthly mortgage payment

The benefits of a repayment plan include:

- Getting current on your mortgage and resolving your delinquency
- Catching up on your past due payments over an extended period of time
- Damaging your credit less than going through a foreclosure
- Staying in your home and avoiding foreclosure

The last option we'll cover for managing a mortgage that's become unaffordable is forbearance. With this option, you and your mortgage company agree to temporarily suspend or reduce your monthly mortgage payments for a specific period of time.

Forbearance lets you deal with your short-term financial problems—such as job loss, disability, or other unique circumstances—by giving you time to get back on your feet and bring your mortgage current.

After the forbearance period ends, you must repay the amount that was reduced or suspended. However, there are a few options available if you qualify.

You may be able to make a one-time payment for the amount due, known as a reinstatement. Or you may be able to enter into a repayment plan or modification (this was covered in the previous chapter).

There are more options available if you're in the military. Be sure to speak with your mortgage company or a HUD-approved housing counselor to determine your eligibility for various programs designed to help you manage your mortgage.

HUD is short for the U.S. Department of Housing and Urban Development. They have trained professionals who can advise you on preventing foreclosure, buying a home, protecting your credit, and other issues. And best of all, their help is free! You can find a housing counselor at HUD.gov or by calling the Homeowners HOPE™ Hotline at 1-888-995-HOPE (4673).

Paying Down a Mortgage Early

So far in this section we've covered ways to make your mortgage more affordable by refinancing through your lender or the federal program, known as HARP, or by using a mortgage modification, setting up a repayment plan, or requesting forbearance.

In this chapter you'll learn the pros and cons of paying off a mortgage early, and in the next chapter we'll cover specific strategies to eliminate a mortgage faster.

Let's start by reviewing the main advantages of paying off a mortgage early. The most obvious benefit is that reducing the balance of a mortgage allows you to pay it off in less time and pay less interest over the life of the loan.

For example, if you owe $150,000 on a 30-year, fixed-rate mortgage at 5 percent, your monthly payment for principal and interest will be about $800. If you have the mortgage for 30 years, you'll end up paying a total of $140,000 in interest.

But let's say that after making payments for four years, you get a $20,000 windfall and send it to pay down your mortgage. If you keep making the $800 monthly payment, you'll pay off the loan in a total of 23 years instead of 30. Plus, you'll cut the total interest that you have to pay from $140,000 to $98,000—saving about $42,000 in interest over the life of the mortgage.

Additionally, paying down a mortgage ahead of schedule means you'll have more equity, which is the difference between a home's value and what you owe on it. For instance, if your home is worth $200,000 and you owe $150,000, you have $50,000 in equity.

Having more home equity can help you qualify to refinance your mortgage for a lower interest rate or to eliminate paying private mortgage insurance to your lender.

While getting out of debt sooner rather than later is generally a good idea, there are disadvantages to prepaying a mortgage that you should weigh carefully. Always consider your mortgage in the context of your entire financial situation.

The main con to paying down a home loan early is that once you send the money, it's tied up in your property. If you unexpectedly lose your job or have a large expense, you won't be able to get that money back easily, if at all.

Money you send to a mortgage, either as a lump sum or by increasing your monthly payment, may be better spent on chipping away at more expensive, higher-rate debt, such as credit cards, payday loans, or student loans. We'll talk about student loans coming up.

Additionally, you may be losing out on the opportunity to invest your extra money for returns that are higher than the rate you're paying on your mortgage. For instance, investing in a mutual fund that pays you an average annual return of 8 percent is better than paying down a mortgage that costs you 5 percent.

Having a paid-off mortgage is terrific—but not if it would leave you without enough cash or a retirement nest egg. Here are three situations when you should never pay down your mortgage ahead of schedule:

1. You don't have emergency savings.

Before you send one extra dollar to your mortgage, be sure to have plenty of cash in an FDIC-insured savings or money market deposit account. Make it a goal to always keep at least three to six months' worth of living expenses on hand.

Even though you won't earn much interest on your emergency savings, its purpose is to keep you safe if you get into an unforeseen financial hardship. Therefore, if you don't have a healthy emergency fund, don't even think about paying down your mortgage early.

2. You have high-interest debt.

As we've covered, you should never pay down a low-interest debt before a high-interest one.

Tackling high-interest debts first saves you the most money in interest, which allows you to pay off lower-interest debts even faster.

As a general rule, mortgages are cheap money. Right now, a 30-year fixed mortgage costs less than 5 percent, while a rewards credit card charges over 16 percent on average. If you're paying at least 1 percent more than the going rate, contact your lender about refinancing your mortgage at a lower rate.

Additionally, you may be eligible to claim the home mortgage interest tax deduction, making your home loan cost even less on an after-tax basis. You never get a tax break for interest paid on other types of debt (except for a certain amount of student loan interest when you meet income limits).

So why pay down an inexpensive mortgage when you could be using your money to get rid of outrageously high consumer debt or car loans instead?

3. You're not investing for retirement.

Investing for a comfortable retirement is one of the most important financial priorities we have.

Using a tax-advantaged retirement account, such as an IRA (Individual Retirement Account) or a workplace retirement plan (such as a 401(k) or 403(b)) cuts your taxes and turbocharges your savings.

If you're not saving a minimum of 10 percent to 15 percent of your gross income for retirement every month, then putting extra money toward a mortgage is a bad idea. To sum up, always remember that paying down a mortgage ahead of schedule should be your last financial priority.

23

Strategies to Pay Off a Mortgage Faster

In this chapter we'll cover eight strategies to pay off a mortgage faster—if it's a smart financial move for you. As you've learned, when it comes to prioritizing your debt, mortgages are way down on the list because they're relatively inexpensive debt.

While getting rid of any type of debt is ultimately good for your finances, a theme that you've heard me repeat in this book is that paying it off in the right order is essential! Always consider your mortgage in the context of your entire financial situation.

Living mortgage-free may sound good, but the

bottom line is that it's not always the best use of your money. You're much better off saving for emergencies, getting rid of expensive debt, and shoring up your retirement funds before paying off your home ahead of schedule.

Note that if you have a fixed-rate mortgage, paying extra to your principal doesn't change your monthly payment, but it does shorten the term, allowing you to pay it off faster.

So if you're in a good financial situation, here are eight strategies to pay off your mortgage even faster:

1. Make biweekly payments.

Some mortgages offer an accelerated, biweekly payment schedule, which is a great strategy. Biweekly payments aren't magic—they simply take advantage of the fact that there are 13 weeks in each quarter, not 12, and there are 52 weeks in a year, not 48.

By paying one half of your mortgage payment every other week, you end up making one extra full payment each year. This strategy works especially well if you get paid every other week, so the biweekly loan payments occur close to each payday.

Here's an example: Christine has a $160,000, 30-year, fixed-rate mortgage at 6.5 percent interest. Her payment is $1,000 per month, or $12,000 per year. If she keeps that payment schedule, she'll pay a total of about $202,000 in interest over the life of the loan.

But if she makes biweekly payments, she pays half the monthly payment, or $500, every other week. That means she pays a total of $13,000 per year instead of $12,000. Keeping a biweekly schedule reduces Christine's interest expense from about $202,000 to $184,000, saving $18,000. Not to mention that she'd pay off the loan in just over 27 years instead of 30. Brilliant!

Problem is, some lenders may not offer a biweekly payment schedule because they don't want to give up any interest income or deal with the administrative hassle. Instead of applying your payment to principal early, they may just put your money in an escrow account and hold it until they receive your full payment. If that's the case, making biweekly payments won't do you any good.

So check with your lender about the best way to start making biweekly payments. If they make it complicated or charge a big fee, simply use another pay-off strategy that I cover here.

2. Make an extra payment each year.

If you can't get a mortgage lender to apply biweekly payments as you send them, make one extra payment a year that gets fully applied to your principal balance.

Let's say your monthly mortgage payment for principal and interest is $1,200. Divide that over 12 months and save $100 per month. At the end of the year, you've got a nice extra amount to send.

As I previously mentioned, the key is to make sure that extra mortgage payments get applied to your principal, not just set aside for the next payment. Make it clear by putting "apply to principal" in the memo section of your payment.

Or you could pay through an online account with your lender. Most of the big banks, such as Chase and Bank of America, have payment portals where you can easily indicate that extra payments go to your principal balance.

3. Add an extra amount each month.

If you're determined to pay down your mortgage early, every little bit will help. Instead of saving to make an additional large payment once a year, pay an extra amount each month.

Let's say you have a $100,000, 30-year, fixed-rate mortgage at 4.5 percent. If you add an extra $100 to your payment each month, you'd pay it off almost nine years earlier and save over $26,000 in interest.

Find a number that works for you, no matter if it's an extra $10 or $1,000 per month. If you get a raise, send the net increase in your paycheck to your mortgage each month. You won't even miss the money.

4. Apply your windfalls.

While you can pay off your mortgage in a slow, steady way by regularly paying the same amount each month, you don't have to be consistent. There's nothing wrong with sending one big payment when you can.

If you get a bonus at work, a tax refund, or an inheritance, put all of it toward your mortgage one month and then go back to your regular payments.

5. Round up your payments.

If you don't have a lot of extra money to put toward paying off your mortgage early, you could simply round up your monthly payments.

For instance, if your payment is $970, why not just pay $1,000? Again, be sure to indicate that the extra should go toward paying down your principal balance.

6. Set a target pay-off date.

If you have a specific date in mind that you want to be mortgage-free—such as on your 50th birthday, when your kids are finally out of the house, or when you retire—figure out how much extra it will take.

Since the math is complicated, use an online mortgage calculator or the free **Mortgage Loan Calculator** at LauraDAdams.com/debt-toolkit. Enter different amounts of extra payments until the final pay-off date is close to your target.

7. Refinance your mortgage.

One way to pay off a mortgage faster is to refinance at a lower interest rate, for a shorter term, or both. Keep an eye on rates and seriously consider refinancing if they fall at least 1 percent below the rate you're currently paying.

As we covered in a previous chapter, refinancing comes with expenses, so you must be sure that you'll stay in your home long enough to recoup the costs.

If you refinance for a lower rate, you could continue paying your old, higher payment, sending the extra to your principal. The amount you'll save depends on your situation, but it could be thousands and it would probably shave years off your loan term.

If you refinance for a shorter term, such as 15 years, the payments will be higher, so make sure you can afford it. A shorter term significantly cuts the amount of interest you pay in addition to getting you out of debt sooner—but it gives you less flexibility if your financial situation changes.

To get the effect of a shorter term, without the

risk, just make payments as if you had a 15-year loan. That puts you in control, not the lender.

Again, use an online calculator or the **Mortgage Loan Calculator** at LauraDAdams.com/debt-toolkit to find the payment needed to eliminate the loan in the time frame you want.

8. Get rid of private mortgage insurance (PMI).

PMI is charged by lenders when you take out a conventional home loan with less than a 20 percent down payment. But you can request a cancellation after you pay down your mortgage balance to 80 percent of the original value of the property.

If you have a 30-year, fixed-rate loan for $180,000, the PMI could be close to $100 per month. Getting rid of that premium frees up $100 that you could use to pay down your principal instead.

If you have rock-solid finances with emergency savings, insurance, consistent retirement contributions, and no debt besides a mortgage, then I highly recommend using these eight strategies to pay off your mortgage ahead of schedule. But if you're not there yet, don't put the cart before the horse!

In the remaining chapters in this section, we'll turn our attention to reducing another common long-term debt: student loans.

RESOURCE: You can use the free **Mortgage Loan Calculator** (Excel) at LauraDAdams.com/debt-toolkit to see how additional payments change your pay-off date.

Restructuring Student Loans

I know many of you are suffocating under a mountain of student loan debt. Approximately 43 million borrowers, or seven in 10 U.S. graduates, are carrying over $1.25 trillion in student loans. The average debt is at an all-time high, $37,000 per graduate.

No matter if you can afford your student loan payments or are struggling to make them, it's important to know your options. I hope you created a **Personal Financial Statement**, which was covered in section 1. If not, take a moment to download it at LauraDAdams.com/debt-toolkit and create a simple spreadsheet that lists your student loans and their payment terms.

Many graduates have multiple loans from a variety of lenders. So, get familiar with what you owe and who you owe it to. If you're not sure, visit your lenders' websites or review free copies of your credit reports at CreditKarma.com or AnnualCreditReport.com.

Having all your loan accounts and their interest rates and terms listed in one place allows you to see the big picture of your finances and know what to prioritize.

If you have more than one federal student loan, the government can consolidate or combine them into one loan with an interest rate that's a weighted average of all of your rates. A consolidation doesn't reduce the interest rate, but it does give you these benefits:

- Fewer accounts and payments to keep track of each month
- Any older, variable-rate loans are converted into one fixed-rate loan (since 2006 they are all fixed)
- No or minimal fees
- Lower monthly payments, if the length of your payment term is extended

Both students and parents can consolidate education loans; however, you can't combine loans that are in different names. Only loans from the same borrower can be consolidated—even married couples must keep their respective education loans separate.

There are usually minimal fees to do a student loan consolidation, and you can work with any lender you choose.

The major downside to consolidating federal student loans is that you may lose special features or benefits that come with your original loans, such as forgiveness for public service work, forbearance for financial hardship, repayment options, and certain interest rate discounts and rebates. So, always ask potential lenders what loan options you'd give up in a consolidation.

Use the Loan Consolidation Calculator at FinAid.org to compare the monthly savings to the increase in total interest expense over the life of the loan. Carefully analyze the cost of repaying your original loans against the cost of paying for a consolidated loan.

Now, let's talk about private student loans, which come from private lenders instead of the federal government. In general, you can't consolidate federal and private student loans together. However, you can consolidate multiple private loans.

The main difference is that unlike consolidating federal loans, the interest rate on your new private loan is *not* a weighted average of your old loan rates. A private lender will evaluate your current financial information and may give you a lower interest rate—which is actually a refinance.

As you've learned, doing a refinance means that you pay off one or more of your high-interest loans with a new loan that has a lower interest rate. While the federal government offers consolidation, student loan refinancing is only available from private lenders.

Private lenders will evaluate your financial situation for approval. But if your finances and credit are better than when you first got your loan, you may be able to refinance at a lower interest rate, which would allow you to:

- Lower your monthly payments
- Shorten your repayment time so you pay off the debt sooner
- Reduce the total amount of interest you must pay
- Choose a variable interest rate loan, which can be more affordable if you plan to pay off your loan relatively quickly
- Enjoy the benefits of consolidation, including having one simplified monthly bill

When you have lower payments, you can pay more toward your principal balance each month, which pays down your loan faster and allows you to easily save money.

There are private lenders that may refinance both federal and private student loans for as little as 2 percent or 3 percent with repayment terms ranging from five to 20 years.

Every lender's underwriting requirements for refinancing are different, so you need to shop and compare offers from several companies to make sure you get the best deal. If you're not sure where to start, check out my **Online Loan**

Comparison Chart at LauraDAdams.com/debt-toolkit for some of the best places to refinance your student loans.

Finaid.org has a list of federal and private student loan institutions, including lenders that specifically offer consolidation loans. You can also get a consolidation loan directly from the U.S. Department of Education at StudentLoans.gov.

RESOURCE: For up-to-date places to refinance student loans, shop and compare options on the free **Online Loan Comparison Chart** (PDF) at LauraDAdams.com/debt-toolkit.

More Strategies for Managing Student Loans

If you have student loans that you want to whittle down faster, without doing a consolidation, there are several options.

Here are six more ways to make your federal and private student loans more affordable:

1. Make accelerated loan payments.

A secret weapon you can use to whittle down your balances on student loans (or any type of loan) faster and pay less interest without paying an extra dime is to make accelerated or biweekly payments instead of monthly payments.

This strategy works for all types of installment loans, if they don't impose a prepayment penalty (which typically isn't the case for student loans). We covered this concept for mortgages in chapter 22.

Biweekly payments take advantage of the fact that one month out of each quarter has five weeks in it instead of four. There are 13 weeks in each quarter, not 12, and there are 52 weeks in a year, not 48. So it's a sneaky way to get the equivalent of one extra monthly payment made each year.

The additional payment works wonders toward paying down a loan faster, which means you pay less interest over time. This strategy works especially well if you get paid every other week, so you can budget the biweekly loan payment to occur close to each payday.

2. Pay more than the minimum.

If you have extra money each month, you could pay more than the minimum payment. Let's say you owe $50,000 at a 5 percent interest rate for 10 years. Your minimum payment would be $530 and cost you about $14,000 in interest over the life of the loan.

But if you pay an additional $100 each month,

you'll save about $3,000 in interest and pay off the loan two years earlier.

When you send more than the minimum payment or make biweekly payments, make sure that you add a note to your payment indicating that you want the extra to go toward your principal balance. Otherwise the lender may think that you're prepaying the next month's payment and simply hold it, which won't help you get rid of the debt any faster.

3. Use windfalls to pay down debt.

As tempting as it can be to quickly spend a bonus, gift, or tax refund on a luxury item, remember that using a windfall to pay down debt is the absolute easiest and most effective way to get rid of debt faster.

When you get a raise or promotion at work, consider it a windfall as well, and make sure you use additional income to accomplish important goals like building an emergency fund, saving for retirement, or paying down debt.

As you've learned, I recommend attacking your highest-interest debt first because it's costing you the most. If you have debts with higher interest rates than your student loans, such as credit cards, personal loans, or payday loans, always pay off those first.

4. Explore loan forgiveness programs.

Some types of federal student loans come with a forgiveness program that allows some or all of your debt to be eliminated. This might be the case if you work full-time in certain industries, such as teaching or medicine, or if you do public service work for a certain amount of time.

However, be aware that some types of forgiven student debts are considered income, so you may still be on the hook for taxes on amounts you don't repay. For example, if you earn $40,000 and have $10,000 of student loan debt forgiven, you'd owe income tax on $50,000 instead of $40,000 that year. So make sure you understand the future tax consequences for any forgiveness programs.

5. Find out if your employer has student loan benefits.

Helping workers to pay down their student loans is an innovative benefit offered by some large companies. Check with your human resources department to find out what may be available.

If your company hasn't created a student loan repayment benefit, propose it as a solution to stay competitive, retain the best talent, and help workers reduce financial stress.

6. Automate your loan payments.

Many lenders offer to automate loan payments by drafting them from your bank account on a given day each month. They know you're less likely to miss a payment this way. But in exchange, your lender may offer a slightly lower interest rate, which helps you pay off your student loans a little bit faster.

Your options depend on the type of loan you have—and you can learn more at StudentLoans.gov. Just remember that if you reduce your monthly student loan payment or lengthen the repayment period, that increases the amount of interest you pay over time.

When you borrow from the government to pay for school, they expect you to pay the loan back on time every month. Defaulting on a federal student loan is very serious because the feds can use everything in their power to collect money from you, including garnishing your wages, keeping your tax refunds, and withholding benefits, such as Social Security retirement payments.

So, if you ever find that you can't make a student loan payment, contact your lender to explain your situation before they're forced to contact you.

And finally, if you have a lot of student loans, don't get anxious about them, simply make smart decisions about how to handle them going forward. Taking control of your debt is ultimately what gives you power over it.

SECTION V

Dealing With Old Debt

Understanding the Statute of Limitations for Debt

In this section, you'll learn smart ways to deal with any old debt you may have. It's probably hurting your credit, well-being, and happiness, so it's time to address it head-on!

In this chapter we'll review what the statute of limitations for debt is and why it should play a role in how you handle an old debt.

The statute of limitations is a legal term that refers to the time period when some legal action may be taken. In other words, it's a strict deadline for filing a lawsuit.

There's a statute of limitations for how long a debt collector or creditor can bring legal action against you to recover certain types of unpaid debts. It varies depending on the state where you live, what's specified in your credit contract, and the type of debt you have.

For example, the statute of limitations for credit card debt may be as long as 10 years in a few states, but most are in the range of three to six years. And some types of debts, such as federal student loans and income taxes, don't have a statute of limitations because you're *never* off the hook for them.

After the statute of limitations on a debt expires, it's considered a time-barred debt. However, in most states, a debt collector can still attempt to collect a time-barred debt from you for as long as they want. They can call you and send you letters—within legal limits, of course.

What you need to know is that even if the statute of limitations has expired on an old debt, a court may still rule against you if you don't appear and use the statute of limitations as your defense. So you should never ignore a lawsuit for an unpaid debt. It's still your responsibility to prove that the statute of limitations has expired and that there's been no activity on an old account.

What Is Reviving or Re-Aging an Old Debt?

What's really tricky about the statute of limitations on debt is that there are different rules for when it starts and stops.

For instance, in some states the statute of limitations begins when you first become delinquent. In others, the clock restarts at day one any time you take an action on the account. This might include simply acknowledging that an old debt is yours, promising a payment, entering into a payment agreement, or making a payment.

Reviving or re-aging an old debt means that you've restarted the statute of limitations and now the collector can sue you for the full amount. That could put you in a worse position than if you hadn't taken any action to begin with.

That's why it's so important to know the law in your state or to consult with an attorney before speaking to a debt collector about an old debt or making a partial payment.

How Long Old Debt Stays on Your Credit Report

When it comes to unpaid debt, be sure you don't confuse the statute of limitations with the length of time that it stays on your credit reports. These are two completely different time limits and are often misunderstood.

The length of time an account with any negative information, such as late payments or being in collections, stays on your credit reports is generally seven years. The exceptions are certain types of bankruptcies, which can remain in your credit file for up to 10 years.

So even if you pay off a delinquent debt or the statute of limitations expires, most debt will not be removed from your credit report until seven years after the date it first became past due.

In the next chapter we'll cover different options you have to manage old debt.

RESOURCE: My online class on credit, ***Build Better Credit—The Ultimate Credit Score Repair Guide*** at LauraDAdams.com/debt-toolkit, is a terrific tool for improving your credit scores and achieving your financial goals.

Should You Settle Old Debt or Pay It in Full?

In this chapter you'll learn four options for managing old, time-barred debt. It's wise to weigh the options carefully for settling for less than you owe or paying in full.

If you have several old debts or have a large past due balance, I recommend speaking with an attorney who understands the law in the state where you live, before choosing one of the following four options:

1. Pay off a debt in full.

Even if the statute of limitations has expired on an old debt, you may still decide to pay it. Many people believe that they have a moral obligation to pay their debts, even after struggling through a financial hardship.

I can't make that decision for you, because everyone's life and financial situation is different. You're the only one who really knows if you truly can or can't afford to pay a debt.

When it comes to your credit reports, as we covered in the previous chapter, paying off an old debt doesn't make its history disappear. An account less than seven years old will remain on your report, even if it's paid in full. However, the current status changes from "unpaid" to "paid," which can help improve your credit.

2. Settle a debt for less than you owe.

If you want to pay a debt but don't want to pay the full amount, many collectors are willing to settle for less. For instance, if you owe $10,000, you might offer to pay $6,000 in one lump sum or $8,000 over time in a series of payments.

The creditor is likely to negotiate as high a settlement as possible, so always start with a low initial offer. Then make sure you get the agreed-upon terms in writing *before* you make any payment.

A settlement agreement should state that your partial payment settles the entire debt in full and releases you from any further obligation. If you don't get this in writing first, your payment could be considered a partial payment, reviving the statute of limitations in some states.

When you settle a debt, the account will show as "settled" on your credit report for the remainder of its seven-year history. This indicates that the debt was not paid in full, as originally agreed, and will have a negative effect on your credit scores.

So remember that settling a debt is better for your credit than leaving it unpaid, but it's not as good as paying it off in full.

3. Make a partial payment on a debt.

If your financial situation has changed for the better, you may decide to begin making payments on an old debt. As we covered in the previous chapter, it's critical to remember that in some states, paying any amount of a time-barred debt restarts a brand new statute of limitations period. That means you give up your legal protection because the collector would be able to sue you in order to recover the full amount of debt.

Your credit report will always indicate that a debt was delinquent or went into collections, even if you begin making payments. However, once you pay it off and the account status shows "paid," your credit has a chance to improve.

4. Pay nothing on a debt.

If you don't pay a debt, you still owe it even after the statute of limitations expires or it falls off your credit reports. That means a collector can continue to contact you indefinitely to try to collect it, even if they can't sue you.

Having an unpaid debt on your credit report is obviously very bad for your credit. So, you need to consider both the statute of limitations and your credit when deciding how to handle an old debt.

Also, understand how easy it could be to inadvertently revive an old debt and give a creditor much more time to file a lawsuit against you. For these reasons, I encourage you to get legal help so you can consider all your options for unpaid debt and make the best decision for your financial future.

Visit USA.gov to find your state's attorney general website and statute of limitations.

5 Debt Collections Rights You Should Know

In this chapter you'll learn the best ways to deal with debt collectors no matter if they contact you due to a mistake or a financial hardship. Knowing your rights is the best way to prevent debt collections harassment.

Many people don't realize that there are federal and state laws that debt collectors—such as collections agencies and attorneys—must follow. The main federal law for personal debt is called the Fair Debt Collection Practices Act (FDCPA). It prohibits debt collectors from harassing you, even when you owe money.

Illegal harassment includes the following:

- Threatening harm or violence
- Calling you repeatedly
- Using obscene or profane language
- Misrepresenting personal or company identity
- Saying or doing anything deceptive or misleading
- Threatening to contact your employer about a debt

Debt collectors also can't contact you at unusual times or places. For instance, they can't call you before 8:00 in the morning or after 9:00 at night. Nor can they call you at work if they've been informed that you're not allowed to take calls there.

Here are five additional debt collections rights to know:

1. You can tell collectors not to contact you.

If you request in writing that a debt collector stop contacting you, then they must heed your request. However, simply telling a collector to back off doesn't prevent them from reporting a delinquency to the credit bureaus or filing a lawsuit against you.

No matter what, a collector is allowed to contact you to send verification of your debt or to inform you about any specific legal action that they intend to take against you.

2. You can dispute debts with collectors.

If you don't believe that you owe all or part of a debt, you can dispute it. However, you've got to put a dispute in writing within 30 days of receiving a collections notice.

Send a certified letter to the collector requesting more information and a formal verification of the debt. When you do this, the collector can't contact you until they provide this information in writing.

3. Collectors can't tell others about your debt.

A debt collector generally isn't allowed to discuss your debt with anyone else, except your spouse or attorney. And if you have an attorney, a collector must contact him or her about your debt, not you.

A collector can only contact other people to find out general information about you, like your phone number or address.

4. You control which debt collectors pay.

If you owe more than one debt, a collector must apply your payments to the debt you choose. In other words, a collector can't use your money to pay a debt that you don't believe you owe.

5. Collectors can't inflate what you owe.

Debt collectors are prohibited from piling on additional interest, fees, or other charges to the amount you owe. However, if you signed a contract that permits additional charges, then they're allowed. So be sure to do the math and verify amounts that a collector is trying to get from you before you send any payments.

Debt Collection and Lawsuits

When you begin communicating with a debt collector, keep good records, such as the date, time, notes of the conversation, and anything you believe may be considered illegal harassment. This documentation will help you if you can't resolve a dispute or end up going to court.

If a collector sues you, don't ignore them—even if you know it's a mistake. You must respond, either personally or through an attorney, by the date on the lawsuit paperwork in order to preserve your rights.

Likewise, if you've been harassed by a debt collector, you can sue them in state or federal court within one year. If you win the case, the collector may have to pay you for damages and court costs.

In the next chapter, you'll learn what zombie debt is and more tips to protect your rights.

29

Facts About Zombie Debt That Can Haunt You

A zombie debt is a debt that's very old or is outside of its statute of limitations—but has come back from the dead to haunt you. It's a funny term—but not a situation to be taken lightly.

Zombie debt comes alive when a collections agency purchases it from the original creditor or from another debt collector for pennies on the dollar. The collector attempts to get you to pay the debt, sometimes using aggressive techniques.

In a previous chapter, you learned that there are rules that allow the statute of limitations to revive or restart at day one, which is known as re-aging an old debt. And believe me, debt collectors have strategies to trick or persuade you to take certain actions that reset the clock, putting you back at square one, so they're allowed to sue you for the full amount owed.

For instance, in some states, the statute of limitations clock restarts any time you take an action on an old debt. The action could be something as simple as acknowledging that an old debt is yours, promising to make a payment, agreeing to a payment plan, or making a payment—no matter how small.

How to Stay Safe From Zombie Debt Collectors

To stay safe from potentially harmful zombie debt collectors, you need to be aware of common tactics:

Verbally harassing you. This is illegal according to the federal Fair Debt Collection Practices Act (FDCPA).

Misrepresenting their company. Collectors can't tell you that they are an attorney or a litigation firm when they aren't.

Threatening a lawsuit. This is illegal if the

statute of limitations for your debt expired, but it can scare people into paying.

Beginning a lawsuit. Collectors may try to sue you even when the statute of limitations has expired. If you receive a summons, don't ignore it, because you have a limited amount of time to respond. If you don't respond in time, you may forfeit your right to fight the lawsuit, using the statute of limitations as your defense.

Getting you to pay for someone else's debt. In general, you're not responsible for debt that's not in your name. The only exception may be the debt of a deceased spouse if you live in a community property state. If a creditor tricks you into believing that you owe a debt that isn't yours, making a payment could be construed as an admission that the debt is yours.

Promising to stop contacting you in exchange for a small payment. As I mentioned, that can be a setup to revive your debt and reset the clock on the statute of limitations so they can sue you for the full amount.

Promising to keep the debt off your credit report. As we've covered, past due debt stays on your credit reports for seven years, even if you settle or pay it off.

So, if a collector contacts you by phone, ask for the company name and address and say you will only communicate through the mail, and then hang up. Don't admit that you owe the debt or engage in conversation or debate about the issue.

Speaking with a collector is risky because you could accidentally say something that gives them a leg up or resets your debt. All communication should be done through snail mail so you have hard copies.

You have the right to request verification of the debt by sending a certified letter back to the creditor within 35 days after receiving their first letter. They must prove that you owe the debt and that they're authorized to collect it.

Again, I encourage to you to get legal help so you can consider all your options for unpaid debt and make the best decision for your financial future.

In the next chapter, you'll learn what to do if you accidentally slip up and make a late payment on a credit account.

30

Tips to Minimize Damage From a Late Payment

Whether it's because your bank account is low, you forgot, or the mail was late, missing a due date on a credit card or loan feels terrible. If you don't take quick action, a late payment can negatively affect your finances for years to come.

In this chapter, you'll learn what happens when you make a late payment and tips to minimize the potential damage.

How Late Payments Affect Your Credit

If there's one thing I hope you've learned so far, it's that not paying a credit account on time is a major offense in the financial world. It's actually *the single most important factor* that credit scoring models use to calculate your scores. I call payment history "the king of credit" because it's so important.

Having late payments or accounts in collections are serious red flags that you haven't been financially responsible and that you may not repay debts with regularity or at all. The consequences are stiff. Even making just one late payment can drastically reduce your scores, especially if you have good or excellent credit.

Other Ways Late Payments Cost You

Once you make a late payment, merchants become wary because it could be a sign that you're in financial trouble and will miss more due dates. So, in addition to having a bad mark added to your credit file, lenders penalize you directly in several different ways.

One is charging a late fee. How much a creditor can tack on to your next statement depends on the agreement or application you signed and the state where you live. Credit card late fees generally range up to $35 and apply the first day you're late.

Car loans and mortgages usually come with a grace period of 10 or 15 days, after which you get charged a fee that could be 4 percent or 5 percent of the overdue payment. If you continue to miss due dates, you'll pile hundreds of dollars on top of the amount you already owe.

With credit cards, another penalty you typically face after paying late for two consecutive months is an increase in your annual percentage rate (APR), up to 29.99 percent. And by the way, that crazy-high rate will be applied to your entire outstanding balance, not just to future charges. Additionally, you might lose accrued credit card rewards or a 0 percent interest promotional offer.

What Does Having an Account in Collections Mean for Your Credit?

If your payment is more than 180 days past due, your creditor may sell your debt to a collector. Then the collections company will attempt to get the overdue balance and fees from you.

Having a debt in collections is much more serious than having a 30- or 60-day late notice on your credit report and causes a bigger dip in your scores. Just like with a late payment, an account in collections stays on your report for seven years from the date you first became delinquent, even after you pay it off.

While you can't make a valid bad debt disappear from your record, paying it shows creditors that you honored your financial obligation. How much a bad debt hurts your credit depends on factors such as what your scores were before the bad mark and the amount of debt you didn't pay.

However, as you make on-time payments and add positive data to your credit reports, the impact of late payments or an account in collections lessens with time.

Tips to Minimize Damage From a Late Payment

Use these four tips to minimize damage from a late payment:

1. Act quickly to settle your account.

The sooner you pay the bill, the better your chance of squeaking by without any fees or rate penalties. The good news is a delinquency can't be reported to the nationwide credit bureaus until 30 days after the due date.

If you get caught up before 30 days, your mistake won't show up on your credit file; however, the creditor can still charge the fees I just covered if you miss a due date. If you don't get caught up quickly and a late payment is reported on your credit file, it can stay there for up to seven years. On the flip side, your on-time payments and all good marks stay on your credit record for 10 years.

If a creditor pegs you as late, but it's in error, dispute it with the credit bureaus right away. Inaccurate or unverifiable information must be removed by law. However, if you were at fault for a late payment, the creditor is under no obligation to retract it, even if you eventually paid up. The purpose of your credit file is to reflect an accurate history of your account activity.

2. Contact the creditor.

If you get your past due account settled but are disappointed to get charged a late fee, contact the creditor to discuss it. If your payment was late by accident, such as getting lost in the mail, explain the situation and ask to have the fee credited.

Lenders and card companies typically want to keep good customers happy, so they may do you a favor—especially if you're polite on the phone. Remember that customer service representatives have a lot of leeway, but they won't be keen to help you if you're in a panic or are rude.

3. Pay all your credit accounts on time.

If your credit scores went down or you got hit with a high penalty APR after a late payment, be extra cautious about never being late again. If you make six months of on-time credit card payments, your issuer is required to reset your interest rate back to the pre-penalty rate.

Plus, your credit scores will slowly improve as you build a history of positive information and the late payment ages. Credit models tend to favor new data more than old entries, so be vigilant about staying on track.

4. Set up automatic reminders.

If you made a late payment because you don't have a good system for paying bills, now's the time to get organized. You could use a spreadsheet, calendar reminders, or smartphone app like Mint.com or Evernote.com.

Many financial institutions allow you to create email or text notifications to remind you about an upcoming payment due date. This is a great way to make sure a deadline never slips past you.

One strategy to make sure that you never miss a minimum credit card payment is to set it up to pay automatically. Even making the minimum payment helps you build credit. You don't get "extra credit" for paying more, but it's wise to pay your balance in full each month so you don't have to pay any interest the next month.

Few people (including me) can say they've never missed a payment due date. It's not fun to slip up and get penalized for it, but it's not the end of the world, either. Don't beat yourself up—just minimize the damage and consider it a learning experience.

In the next section, we'll cover tips and strategies to manage money stress so you can build a financial life you love.

SECTION VI

Managing Money Stress

31

7 Strategies to Reduce Money Stress

Many people mistakenly believe that if they just had *more* money, all their stress would disappear and they could finally be happy. In some cases, earning more is the solution to improving your financial health or dealing with a hardship.

But what's surprising is that you can feel anxious about your financial situation no matter how much you make. Oftentimes, having more money just causes you to inflate your lifestyle in a way that doesn't reduce stress or bring you more long-term happiness.

In this chapter, you'll learn what's at the root of money stress and seven strategies to reduce it so you build a financial life you love.

What Causes Money Stress

Stress is nothing more than your body's response to a situation or a series of events. Think about a stressful situation, such as hearing the fire alarm go off in your office building or seeing a tornado approach your neighborhood.

Some people react by hyperventilating; other people stay completely calm and in control. The situation is the same for everyone, but the way each person perceives the situation is very different.

There are a few common stressors that can cause money stress. Understanding and avoiding them is the secret to achieving more with less anxiety.

One widespread problem is living above your means, which is when living expenses exceed your income. You finance your lifestyle using some form of debt, such as a credit card or loan. Or you might drain your savings or retirement account to pay your bills.

If your finances go in the red every month, or if you're living paycheck to paycheck, you can't get ahead of your expenses and build wealth for the future. Knowing that you're going backwards or just treading water can cause worry and financial stress.

For some people, owing any amount of money can be a source of stress—even if you're meeting your expenses and diligently saving for the future. High earners can feel anxious if they have a complicated financial situation that's gotten out of control. This can happen when you're unorganized, have too many accounts, begin managing your finances for the very first time, or don't have a clear financial plan to achieve your goals.

While money stress may never disappear completely from your life, reducing it as much as possible can improve your relationships, health, and general sense of well-being. Use these seven strategies to stay calm, think clearly, and work on solutions to your financial challenges:

1. Adopt a new money mindset.

For many, financial stress comes from projecting a worst-case scenario into the future. You can exaggerate a situation in your mind to the point that your heart starts pounding and your palms start sweating.

Remind yourself that you're not in the future—you're in the present moment, where you have the power to make a difference. Choices always exist to take control and improve any financial problem.

Actions are always preceded by thoughts and beliefs. So, reframe how you think and speak about your finances.

Never say that you can't increase your income or that you should cut spending. Instead, say *I want to increase my income* or *I will cut my spending*. A shift in your language is the first step to a shift in your mental attitude.

Never believe that a financial challenge is a sign of personal failure or weakness. Whatever your situation, millions of people have struggled with the same thing. You and your family can grow stronger by proactively working through your money challenges.

2. Focus on the positive in your financial life.

Though it may sound cliché, keeping a positive attitude and using positive language can reduce your stress response to financial problems. Instead of dwelling on what's wrong with your finances, think about what's going right that you can be grateful for. I promise whatever your situation, there are many people going through tougher times who would love to switch places with you.

Try keeping a gratitude journal as both an outlet for negative thoughts and a place to write down at least three things you're thankful for each day. *The Five Minute Journal: A Happier You in Five Minutes a Day* or its mobile app version are terrific tools that I've used to build a daily gratitude practice.

3. Radically cut your expenses.

If you're spending too much due to a hardship or because you or someone in your family is a chronic overspender, you're probably seeing your savings dwindle and your credit card debt going up, right along with your anxiety level.

This is a dangerous situation because you can't save if nothing is left over at the end of the month. And if you can't save, you can't get ahead and build wealth.

So, decide what's truly important to you. Then

take control by creating a spending plan and aggressively cutting your expenses.

Can you slash housing costs? This is a difficult but good place to start because it's probably one of your largest expenses. A good rule of thumb is to spend no more than 25 percent of your gross income on a mortgage or rent payment.

If your housing expense is a source of financial stress, take a hard look at downsizing or relocating to a different neighborhood or town. Taking a similar or better job in a less expensive area is another solution to get ahead financially.

Vehicles are another expensive category to cut, when possible. According to Kelley Blue Book, in its first year alone, the average new car depreciates 36 percent.

So, buying a pre-owned vehicle is a much better deal than buying a new one. Also consider other options to save, such as using public transportation, working from home, or moving to an area where you could drive less.

4. Create additional sources of income.

It can be difficult to reach your goals when

you're living paycheck to paycheck and sliding backwards financially. I'll cover more about breaking the paycheck-to-paycheck cycle in the next chapter.

Brainstorm ways to earn more income, such as looking for a higher-paying job, getting a second job, starting your own business, or doing a side gig.

Having multiple streams of income is like an insurance policy. Not only does it help you pay the bills and eliminate debt faster, but it helps you maintain security if one of them dries up.

How can you leverage the skills you already use in your job to create a profitable project or side business? What interests do you have that other people would pay for, such as music, gardening, designing, caring for pets, writing, or tutoring?

5. Stay informed about your finances.

If you delay opening bills because you don't want to deal with them, you're not helping ease your money stress. Open all mail right away and set a current or future payment date for all bills to make sure you never miss a deadline.

Keep track of how much you're spending, how much you're saving, and whether you need to tweak your monthly budget. Check out free apps, such as PersonalCapital.com or Mint.com

6. Take a stress break.

Once you've taken actions such as focusing on the positive, cutting expenses, putting savings on autopilot, and looking for extra income sources, you'll probably feel more in control. But as I mentioned, you may never eliminate all money stress.

If you begin feeling anxious about money, do something healthy to take your mind off your stress. Maybe it's playing with your dog or kids, going for a run, enjoying a hobby, watching a movie, listening to music, or doing yoga.

7. Get professional help.

If you have persistent financial problems that you can't solve on your own, talk to a wise friend, family member, or financial professional. They may help you see options and solutions to financial problems that you're overlooking. That goes a long way toward gaining control and reducing anxiety about any financial challenges.

If debt is the source of your stress, get serious about using the information in this book to pay it off as quickly as possible. A good rule of thumb is to keep the total of all monthly debt obligations below 40 percent of your gross monthly income.

How to Stop Living Paycheck to Paycheck

If you feel like your paycheck is gone the moment you get it, you're not alone. Many people are stuck living paycheck to paycheck and just can't seem to break the cycle.

While escaping this dilemma isn't easy, it's possible to get ahead by changing your mindset, examining your lifestyle, and creating new habits. Once you free up even a small amount of discretionary income each month, it's possible to build a better financial life with more security and less stress.

Use these eight tactics to break the paycheck-to-paycheck cycle for good:

1. Admit you have a challenge to overcome.

To break the cycle of living paycheck to paycheck, first, you must admit that it's a problem, if you haven't already. If you're not setting aside any money, you're in a dangerous position that leaves you vulnerable to unexpected hardships. Any setback can put you in an even worse position than you are in now.

If you don't save for emergencies or your long-term needs, you're not financially grounded—you're simply drifting from one bank deposit to the next. That's a surefire way to devastate your financial life.

Whether the root of your money strain is due to overspending or earning too little, it's time to face it head-on. If you don't act now to break the paycheck-to-paycheck cycle, accumulating a cash reserve or building wealth for retirement simply won't be possible.

If you have a partner or spouse, talk to him or her about making a commitment to turn your financial life around. You might set a goal to build a small emergency fund before the end of the year or contribute to a retirement account every month.

When there's money left over at the end of the month, you have the power to save and pay down debt. Without it, you simply don't have the ability to build financial security.

2. Forget what other people think.

Living paycheck to paycheck is a predicament that can devastate your finances no matter how much you make. Even high earners can let expenses and consumer debt get out of control.

When you want the appearance of success, or feel entitled to have what others have, you're probably living a lifestyle that you can't afford. If you equate your self-image with material things that are draining your bank account, it's time to quit worrying about what other people think.

A poor self-image is a bottomless pit that no amount of spending can fill up or make good. Search for ways to fulfill those emotional needs without spending beyond your means.

Some people were born savers, and others continually struggle to delay gratification. If you can't seem to put a lid on spending, it's time to quit rationalizing bad behavior that's holding you back.

You can only take full control of your finances when you take full control of yourself. For many people, the inability to manage money is really the inability to manage themselves.

So, get comfortable saying "no" to family or friends who may pressure you to spend more than you should. Get focused on goals you want to achieve and don't let anyone prevent you from reaching them.

3. Measure your cash flow carefully.

You can't change what you don't measure, so track your expenses carefully. No matter how much you earn, you must spend less. Again, when you live paycheck to paycheck and spend everything you make, it's impossible to get ahead.

Find a way to keep an eye on spending that's easy for you. It could be jotting down every expense in a paper notebook or entering costs into a computer spreadsheet.

Try free apps, such as PersonalCapital.com or Mint.com, that sync with your financial accounts and automatically pull in your transactions. TillerHQ.com is a Google Sheets—based tool that consolidates your daily financial transactions into a dashboard that you can customize.

Technology makes it easier than ever to create a spending plan and stick to it. So, if you don't have a clue where your money goes every month, get curious. You may be shocked by what you find.

Budgets don't have to be forever, but they're an essential part of taking control of your cash flow and understanding how to cut back. Then you can allocate that savings to build wealth and security for the future.

4. Cut your largest expenses first.

An effective way to stop living paycheck to paycheck is to cut your largest expenses, such as housing, first. A good rule of thumb is to never pay more than 20 percent to 25 percent of your gross income on rent or a mortgage, even if a home lender says you can afford a bigger payment.

You may need a radical lifestyle change to downsize your housing. Consider a variety of options, even if you don't like them. Remember, financial sacrifices will help you get ahead and don't have to be permanent.

If you buckle down for a year, you can accomplish a lot with your money. You could move to a less expensive apartment, home, neighborhood, town, or state. Consider moving in with family or getting a roommate to share expenses.

Vehicles are another budget-buster to evaluate. Driving a used car is always a better deal than buying a new one. Never let your car payment exceed 10 percent of your gross income. And check out other transportation options, such as public transit, carpooling, or using a ride-sharing service.

Keep looking for more big cuts. You've got to take control of your financial life and make serious changes to break the paycheck-to-paycheck cycle and create more financial breathing room.

5. Reduce the cost of debt.

Many people are drowning in expensive debt that keeps them locked in the paycheck-to-paycheck habit. Can you refinance your mortgage for a lower interest rate or sell your home and move into a less-expensive one?

Shaving the interest off high-rate credit cards and loans can add up to big savings. Consider consolidating debt using a low-rate personal loan so you have more money available every month. As you've learned in this book, shifting debt to a lower-rate product is a wise way to save interest and pay off debt faster.

6. Automate savings (even small amounts).

No matter your financial goals, automation is the trick to making saving easy. Moving money into a dedicated savings account, before you have a chance to spend it, makes it more likely that you'll meet your goals.

If you have a workplace account, such as a 401(k) or 403(b), they offer built-in automation because contributions can only come from your paycheck. Always participate and contribute at least enough to max out any employer matching. Make small increases every year until you're contributing at least 15 percent of your gross income.

Don't have a 401(k) or 403(b) at work? No

problem—you can automate contributions from your bank account to an IRA or an account for the self-employed, such as a Solo 401(k) or a SEP-IRA.

Also work on building an emergency fund at the same time. Having just a few hundred dollars set aside can reduce stress if you have an unexpected expense. Ideally you should work up to having three to six months' worth of living expenses in a bank savings account.

It's okay to start small. Even if you can only set aside $25 a month for savings and $25 for retirement, you'll be surprised how quickly balances can grow over time. Treat savings like mandatory bills that you owe yourself and automate them when possible.

Using your money to create a secure financial future, instead of spending it on material possessions, will give you a feeling of freedom that expensive toys never deliver. You can reduce stress by purchasing less stuff that you really don't need and making a commitment to save at least 10 percent of your income.

7. Create more ways to make money.

Cutting unnecessary expenses is great for breaking the paycheck-to-paycheck cycle, but earning more can be the ticket to turning your financial life around. You could:

- Get a second job
- Pick up extra hours at work
- Ask for a raise
- Seek a promotion
- Start a side hustle

There are many ways to create more income streams, such as driving for a ride-share service, house-sitting, dog walking, tutoring, delivering groceries for Instacart.com, or writing. Try something new. You likely have skills that can be used in a variety of jobs and types of work.

8. Focus on the future lifestyle you want.

If you're like me, you want security and financial freedom, which are impossible to get when you're trapped living paycheck to paycheck. Instead of hoping that next month will be different from this month, focus on the future you want to create.

Nothing worthwhile is easy to achieve. So,

decide today how you want your life to be in five, 10, or 20 years from now. The moment you create a plan and begin taking small action steps, you'll feel much less stress and instability.

In the next and final chapter, you'll learn simple micro habits you can incorporate into daily life to improve your finances.

Micro Habits That Create Financial Success

Daily habits lay the foundation for short- and long-term success with our health, wealth, and happiness; therefore, it's critical to carefully examine our repetitive behaviors and thought patterns. They're either moving you closer to your goals or farther away from them.

I'll admit that breaking old habits and forming new, beneficial ones isn't easy. But one way to create more financial success is to begin layering simple micro habits into your routine that require minimal effort and motivation to complete.

You already have many tiny daily habits, such as brushing your teeth or taking vitamins. Any small step that allows you to stop a negative habit or start a positive one is a micro habit. They take up little time, but they can build up to huge, significant results when you make them part of your routine.

Try using these seven micro habits to live a richer life:

1. Listening to 15 minutes of audio.

Everyone has 15 minutes of daily downtime, such as when you get dressed, shave, put on makeup, fold clothes, take a lunch break, or commute. That's the perfect opportunity to listen to a great podcast or audiobook that improves your life.

No matter if you're an employee or have a business or side gig, find audio content about your industry so you can stay up-to-date. Or seek topics like customer service, e-commerce, or marketing to find more customers and serve clients at a higher level. Choose anything you want to start doing better and find expert content that moves you forward with information and motivation.

The beauty of podcasts and audiobooks is that

you can consume portions when you have small windows of time and then pick up where you left off. Start by listening to something new that interests you for just 15 minutes and see how you can incorporate it into your day on a regular basis. Some people enjoy listening at a faster speed, such as 1.5 or 2 times the regular audio, to hear more content.

When you surround yourself with positive information, it's easier to stay informed and inspired. You never know where the information may take you. Listening is a fun way to make small, incremental life changes that make you a little bit better every day.

2. Reading one page of a book.

With so much digital and social media fighting for our attention, making time to read physical books can seem daunting. But reading the old-fashioned way has so many benefits that you don't get from reading on a device.

Reading electronic text can slow you down a bit compared to the speed at which you read a real book. Feeling the paper and flipping pages also creates a deeper sensory experience that helps reading comprehension and remembering what you read.

Create a micro habit to read just one book page a day. While this might seem like a ridiculously tiny goal, that's the point. If you read one page, it's likely that you'll read several—but it's okay if you don't. Taking a long time to read a book is better than not reading one at all.

Build this micro habit into your early morning or nighttime routine. I love snuggling up with a good book to relax before going to sleep. Getting engrossed in a great book can help you learn, reduce stress, and be a signal to your brain that it's time to wind down.

Check out the **Recommended Reading List** at LauraDAdams.com/debt-toolkit for my favorite personal finance and productivity books.

3. Going to bed 30 minutes earlier.

Your health lays the foundation for what you can achieve with your money and life. If you're not taking care of your body, your mind will also suffer. In addition to maintaining a good diet and regular exercise, try going to bed 30 minutes earlier.

That extra time might allow you to read a book before drifting off or get a better night's sleep. I love watching TV with my husband after dinner, but I try to set a limit of one hour or two. As fun as it can be to stay up late watching your favorite TV shows, it's probably not helping you achieve your goals.

Instead, begin your bedtime routine a little earlier so you can wake up feeling recharged, focused, and able to accomplish more. You only have one life, so don't make a habit of wasting time.

4. Buying quality instead of quantity.

A micro habit to pare down your possessions and enjoy them more is to buy less stuff, but choose higher-quality items. It's easy to get in the trap of buying lots of clothes, shoes, or home furnishings because they're on sale or seem like an irresistible "bargain" in the moment.

I love a sale as much as the next person, but I find that when I buy higher-quality items, I cherish and take better care of them than I do for cheap stuff. I use a "one in, one out" rule that forces me to sacrifice a similar item when I buy something new.

For example, if I buy running shoes, I need to sacrifice an old pair. Got a new top or pair of jeans? I must pick one that I haven't worn in the past year to donate to charity.

Sometimes I push myself to get rid of two items for each one that I add to my clothes closet, kitchen, or bookshelves to make sure I'm slowly cutting down, instead of accumulating. This is more of a mindset shift than a daily habit, but it can really transform the way you spend money on material possessions.

5. Setting a spending waiting period.

In addition to buying less, creating a rule that you must wait a minimum of 24 hours before buying anything over a certain amount, such as $50 or $100, is a key micro habit for financial success. By "sleeping on it," you decide with a clear mind if buying a discretionary item is a need, or just a random impulse purchase. Often, you'll have a change of heart and realize you didn't need or want it anyway.

If you're shopping in a brick-and-mortar store

and find something you want over your price limit, take a picture of it and its price. You can revisit the item at least 24 hours later and even take the time to do comparison shopping online.

6. Automating savings.

As I previously mentioned, automating your money is a powerful tip for success. Make it a micro habit for savings and investments. The idea is that what you don't see in your bank account, you can't spend.

It's okay to start small. Even investing $50 a month is better than nothing. If you invested that much for 40 years and earned a conservative 6 percent return, you'd have $100,000.

Creating your accounts and setting the savings automation infrastructure is what's most important to build wealth and move your finances in a positive direction.

7. Saying "no" more often.

Saying "no" to negative people or invitations that don't align with your goals is a wise micro habit to develop. It can be much harder to do the right things when you're around other people's drama and conflicts.

The people you surround yourself with have a major influence over who you become. So, don't let negative influences penetrate your mind. Stay true to who you are and what you want to accomplish.

Instead of acting unconsciously and being jerked around by unproductive impulses, use these tiny habits to ease into a new world of positive behaviors and outcomes.

RESOURCE: Subscribe to the free ***Money Girl podcast*** at LauraDAdams.com/debt-toolkit for weekly advice and inspiration to take your personal finances to the next level.

Also see the **Recommended Reading List** for the 49 best personal finance and productivity books.

Maintaining Your Momentum

Just like losing a lot of weight doesn't happen overnight, getting out of debt won't happen quickly, either. It's a part of making a commitment to a new and improved lifestyle. It's a part of accepting new beliefs about money and adopting better financial habits that you follow every day.

You begin to take control of your financial reality when you can take full control of yourself —not a moment before. The inability to manage money is actually the inability to manage yourself.

Remember that being rich or wealthy is a relative

concept. The absolute amount of money you have isn't nearly as important as how you handle your money each and every day.

Put your full attention on these solutions:

- Increasing your income
- Decreasing your fixed and variable expenses
- Increasing your emergency savings
- Increasing your investments
- Optimizing your debts so they cost you less by refinancing, modifying, consolidating, or using balance transfer cards when it's prudent
- Negotiating for debt settlements when possible
- Paying down your debts, starting with the most dangerous and expensive ones
- Automating your savings and extra debt payments so they're paid first
- Creating long-term financial goals that motivate you
- Simplifying your lifestyle

No matter if you're a millionaire with money

freely flowing, or if you're making minimum wage, you have the power and ability to set aside enough money to create financial security. Making the most of what you have, and being grateful for it, is truly the secret of financial well-being and happiness.

If I had to sum up the essence of this book or one key way to reduce your debt, it would be this: You must widen the gap between the money you make and the money you spend. The difference is what will get you out of debt and keep you out of debt for good.

I want to thank you for reading or listening to this book and encourage you to continue learning about personal finances. Try to immerse yourself in financial topics that you know the least about. Of course, the *Money Girl* podcast is a great way to do that. Not only is the show concise and free, but I'll always give you the most up-to-date and relevant financial information.

Here's to living your best debt-free life!

* * *

Thank you for reading or listening to *Debt-Free Blueprint*. If you found it helpful for taking control of your finances and getting out of debt, I would really appreciate you submitting a book review at LauraDAdams.com/debt-toolkit.

About the Author

Laura D. Adams is an award-winning author of multiple books, including *Money Girl's Smart Moves to Grow Rich*. She's been the host of the popular *Money Girl* podcast, a top weekly audio show in Apple Podcasts, since 2008.

Laura is a frequent source for the national media and has been featured on most major news outlets, including NBC, CBS, ABC FOX, Bloomberg, NPR, the *New York Times*, the *Wall Street Journal*, the *Washington Post*, *Money*, *Time*, *Kiplinger's*, *Business Insider*, *USA Today*, *U.S. News*, *Huffington Post*, *Marketplace*, *Forbes*, *Fortune*, *Consumer Reports*, MSN, and many other radio, print, and online publications.

Millions of readers and listeners benefit from Laura's practical financial advice. Her mission is to empower consumers to live richer lives through her writing, speaking, spokesperson, teaching, and advocacy work.

Laura received an MBA from the University of Florida. She lives in Austin, Texas, with her husband.

- twitter.com/lauraadams
- bookbub.com/profile/laura-d-adams

Copyright © 2018 by Laura D. Adams

All rights reserved.

ISBN-13: 978-1-7237-1974-5

No part of this book may be reproduced in any form or by any electronic or mechanical means, including information storage and retrieval systems, without written permission from the author, except for the use of brief quotations in a book review.

Made in the USA
Columbia, SC
06 December 2018